D0439834

The Bad Girl's Guide to Getting What You Want

The Bad Girl's

Guide to Getting What You Want

by Cameron Tuttle

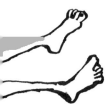

Illustrations by Susannah Bettag

CHRONICLE BOOKS
SAN FRANCISCO

Bad Girl's Guide™ and Bad Girl Swirl™ are trademarks
of Bad Girl Swirl, Inc.

Library of Congress Cataloging-in-Publication Data available.

ISBN 0-8118-2896-4

Printed in the United States of America.

Designed by Pamela Geismar

Distributed in Canada by Raincoast Books
9050 Shaughnessy Street
Vancouver, British Columbia V6P 6E5

10 9

Chronicle Books LLC
85 Second Street
San Francisco, California 94105

www.chroniclebooks.com

I want validated parking for the rest of my life. I want to hear the sound of the

Acknowledgments

I wanted help writing this book. And I got it—thank God! Thanks to every clever person I talked to, thought about, or happened to pass on the street while frantically writing. My deep-dish gratitude to the brainstormers, the hand-holders, and the bar sisters, especially Cate Corcoran, Julie Mason, Shannon Kelley, Katharine Armstrong, Julie Caskey, Gretchen Carter, Hilary Redmond, Amy Robinson, Halle Becker, Judy Johnson, and Leslie Kirby. Good girls and bad, I hope you all know how much I appreciate your help.

Many thanks to the patient, talented professionals who gracefully made up for my bad sense of time: Susannah Bettag, Kate Chynoweth, Pamela Geismar, and Jay Schaefer.

Special thanks to my agent, Charlotte Sheedy, bad long before it was fashionable; my technical advisors, Matt Waller and Andy Schell; my parole officer, Jane Donut; the Fictional Sluts for putting up with me even though this is the only fiction I've written all year; and the Honeywell Detective Agency for keeping me safe from myself and all those sweet stalkers. Case closed.

Introducing the Out-of-Focus Group Girls, all bad to the bone, whose secret desires run across the bottom of these pages: Mikyla, Andrea, Brenda, Julianne, Donna, Karen, Stacey, Maria, Angela, Erin, Farah, Lisa, Heather, Samantha, Jenn, Lila, Kim, Marcella, Julie, the most fabulous Mimi, Jill, Patti (a.k.a Piddles Lopez), Alicia, Catharine, Tracy, Karla, Patty, Lizi, Diane, Mary, Lola, Kathleen, Karen, Marissa, Angie, Veronica, Eileen, Elaine, Bonnie, Cynthia, Ginny, Merry, Louise, Jane, Stephanie, Kathy, Molly, Aimee, Nicole, Brynn, Terri, Phoebe, Sarah, Anne Marie, Barb, Kortney, Meg, Sara, Tres, Jennifer, Kiki, Debbie, Lorraine, Lynn, Pilar, Joanne, Sabrina, Shaya, Dottie, Dana, Jeanne, Susan, Kate, and Debbie. Thanks to each of you and to everyone else who shared and bared all for this book.

ocean in my shoes.   I want others to describe me as "magnetic."   I want a farm

Contents

A Bad Girl's Wish List

Secret Desires

Bad Girl To-Do List

The Bad Girl Swirl

*B*eing a girl is your ice cream sundae—being a bad girl is the cherry on top.

At every age, being a girl rocks. It's your ace in the hole, your backstage pass, your automatic first-class upgrade. Being a girl is what makes you who you are. It's your power source, your secret sauce, and your *69. Being a girl is the real deal. It's your broadest bandwidth, your badge of honor, and your gift with purpose. Use it with respect—or lose the perks that go with it.

Bad girls make it happen. A bad girl knows what she wants and how to get it. She makes her own rules, makes her own way, and makes no apologies. She knows when to work a room, when to work the angles, and when to work her curves—or do all of the above. A bad girl is everyone's dream date and nobody's fool. She's attitude in overdrive, coast-to-coast confidence, and fast-forward fun. She's your boldest dreams and your inner wild. A bad girl is you at your best—whoever you are, whatever your style.

Note to Self: Smile and wink for your mug shot.

Once you light your badness fuse, you'll start to hear the muse—that sassy little voice inside your head reminding you to go for it, trust your instincts, and find the G-spot of your own life.

filled with animals. I want to enjoy shopping again. I want my cat to respect me.

No matter what you want in this world, your bad girl self is the perfect tool for the job. It's your joystick that gives you control of the action. It's your superhero power. It's your whoopee cushion that keeps you laughing through the long lectures of life. Tapping into your badness is the way to get things done and get things fun.

Note to Self: Say "yes" to things you're not sure you can do. Except bungee jumping without a rope.

When you get really good at being bad and getting what you want, you'll be living in the Bad Girl Swirl—the getting-it zone, that magical place in time where everything comes together and goes your way. When you're in the swirl, you're in your element and in your groove. You're feeling good, you've got the power, you've got your mojo, you're hitting your stride and hitting the sweet spot.

When you're in the swirl, you share the air of every bad girl who's ever lived. You're Cleopatra cruising the Nile, you're Dorothy Parker at the Algonquin, you're Rosa Parks in the front of the bus, and you're Missy Piggy hitting the high notes. You're Aretha getting some respect, you're Tina strutting her stuff, you're Xena kicking some ass. When you're in the swirl, you know what every bad girl knows—being bad feels pretty damn good.

Note to Self: Stop making the same old stupid mistakes and start making new ones.

In Bad Company

Being good won't get you noticed. Check your history books, your CD collection, your memory, or your local cable listing. See any women admired for keeping their mouths shut, batting their eyelashes, or writing perfect thank-you notes? Great women throughout history were

I want the wisdom to know what I really want and the strength to make it happen.

bad girls. They were passionate about what they wanted. They were dreamers, risk-takers, and visionaries who defied the norm of their times. They didn't conform and they didn't take no for an answer. They weren't afraid to break the rules or scare the hell out of men to get what they wanted. You don't have to change the world to find your badness. But you'll definitely change yours.

Note to Self: Why be a gossiper when you can be a gossipee?

What You *Think* Is What You Get

The more you think like a bad girl, the more you'll act like a bad girl. And the more you act like a bad girl, the more you'll feel like a bad girl. It's all just part of the swirl.

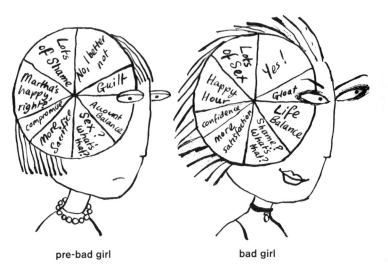

pre-bad girl   bad girl

I want a self-fulfilling roll of toilet paper.   I want to be an urban legend.   I want to

In Bad Company

Bad Girls Making Music
Billie Holiday
Janis Joplin
Josephine Baker
Tina Turner
Bessie Smith
Lil' Kim
Aretha Franklin
Bonnie Raitt
Shania Twain
Eartha Kitt
Courtney Love
Joan Jett
Chaka Khan
Deborah Harry
Sheryl Crow
Melissa Etheridge
Annie Lennox
The Bad Girl formerly
  known as Prince
Liz Phair
Grace Slick
Chrissy Hynde
Stevie Nicks
Queen Latifah

Bad Girls Making Movies
Marilyn Monroe
Miss Piggy
Raquel Welch
Pam Grier
Carrie Fisher
Barbara Stanwyck

Tallulah Bankhead
Drew Barrymore
Callie Khouri
Judy Davis
Marlene Dietrich
Mae West
Sharon Stone
Rita Hayworth
Jane Campion
Christina Ricci
Greta Garbo
Katharine Hepburn
Penny Marshall

Bad Girls Scoring Points
Serena and Venus
  Williams
Mia Hamm
Florence Griffith Joyner
Martina Navratilova
Lisa Leslie
Brandi Chastain
Michelle Akers
Laila Ali

Bad Girls Making History
Eve
Joan of Arc
Harriet Tubman
Amelia Earhart
Eva Perón
Anne Boleyn
Rosa Parks
Shirley Muldowney

Annie Oakley
Queen Elizabeth I
Angela Davis
Wilma Rudolph
Eleanor of Aquitaine
Madeleine Albright
Marie Curie
Jane Goodall
Margaret Sanger
Rosie the Riveter
Martha Graham

Bad Girls Making Literature
Jane Austen
Anaïs Nin
Toni Morrison
George Sand
Dorothy Parker
Edith Wharton
Audre Lorde
Colette
Joan Didion
Susan Sontag
The Brontë sisters
Maya Angelou
Grace Paley

Bad Girls Making Art
Georgia O'Keeffe
Frida Kahlo
Cindy Sherman
Laurie Anderson
Jenny Holzer
Susannah Bettag
Nan Goldin
Guerrilla Girls

Bad Girls Making Us Laugh
Lucille Ball
Gilda Radner
Sandra Bernhard
Lily Tomlin
Roseanne Barr
Holly Golightly
Rosie O'Donnell
Phyllis Diller
Ellen Degeneres
Oprah Winfrey
Lisa Kudrow
Teri Garr
Julia Louis-Dreyfus
Bridget Jones

Bad Girls Who
Make Men Weep
Scarlett O'Hara
Catwoman
Elizabeth Taylor
Heather Locklear
Gloria Steinem

Bad Girls So Bad They
Need Only One Name
Eve
Madonna
Thelma & Louise
Xena
Cleopatra
Eloise
Charo
Colette
Lucy *(Peanuts)*
Ling

Bad Girls We'd Love to See

Donna Weed
Donna Reed stoned

Mary Tighter Moore
*Mary Tyler Moore with
yet another face-lift*

Barfie Doll
Bulimic Barbie

Crap 'n' Pee Gifford
A lifelike Kathie Lee doll

Tripper Gore
Tipper on acid

Sinderella
Cinderella in Barbarella's outfit

Hello Titty
Hello Kitty topless

Little Ho Peep
Little Bo Peep on the streetcorner

Ally McMeal
*Ally McBeal as a fat fast-food
promotion action figure*

Nancy Shrew
Nancy Drew with PMS

Hey, What Do *You* Want?

What do you really want from your life? Are you sure? How do you know? What makes your mouth water? What makes you sweat? Do you want it? Or do you want to run from it?

Most of us have been brainwashed into thinking we want a lot of things, weird things, things we don't even like. We're supposed to want puffy lips, a pretty little nose, a skinny and shapely figure, breasts large enough to nourish a small country, hair in very few, very small, very odd-shaped patches. We're supposed to want a tall, handsome, successful husband, 2.5 children who are gifted but not annoyingly so, a big house, a snazzy car, stock options, and a Prozac-free 100% positive attitude.

We're supposed to want to be great at what we do but not so great that we intimidate anyone. We're supposed to want lots of things for other people but not want too much for ourselves. We're supposed to want to be good girls. Whose lame idea was that?

Note to Self: Good girls do what's expected—bad girls do the unexpected.

By the time we're old enough to make our own choices, most of us don't even know what we want. We've been going with the flow, following the rules, and drinking the Kool-Aid for so long that we've lost touch with our own deepest desires. What's worse—we don't even know that we don't even know what we want.

Note to Self: Do not flush toilet with foot when wearing mules.

cut through the bullshit, get to what matters, and not feel judged. I want to be as

The Desperate Desire Decoder

WHAT YOU THINK YOU WANT	WHAT'S GOING ON FOR YOU	WHAT YOU REALLY WANT
a better boyfriend	you don't feel loved, understood, or appreciated	a better therapist and a puppy
a boob job so you'll have bigger, perkier tits	you're out of touch with your feminine power	a better job with bigger perks
to have an affair	you need to be pampered, caressed, and fawned over with no strings attached	a deep-tissue aromatherapy massage with a sexy masseur once a week
stock options	you think everyone's getting rich except for you	someone to explain how stock options work so you'll know to take the cash instead
an engagement ring with a rock worth at least $30,000	apparently, not much	a sense of self-worth
a baby	all your friends have this cute little accessory and you don't	a grossly overpriced, cute little faux-fur handbag

to eat every chocolate chip cookie within a three-mile radius	vicious PMS	to eat a couple ibruprofen and dance around the room in a thong loving every inch of your jiggling, water-retaining flesh
to spend the entire year complaining to your friends about your crappy life	you've lost perspective	to volunteer at a women's shelter for a year and realize how lucky you really are
a new pair of fabulous shoes	you're feeling needy yet deserving	three new pairs of fabulous shoes
to hit that moron in front of you and run him off the road	road rage	to hit the open road for a road trip
a caring, sensitive man who can talk about his emotions	you want to be in a relationship with an equal partner	a girlfriend
anything Prada	all your friends are doing it	new friends
another grossly overpriced, cute little faux-fur handbag	you're reading too many fashion magazines	a baby

A Typical Good Girl's Transformation

Once you go bad, you'll never go back.

	MONDAY	WEDNESDAY	FRIDAY
Awakened by:	Recurring anxiety dream	Recurring sex dream	Recurring sex
First thought of the day:	I'm already late.	I'm already happy.	I'm so happy I don't care if I'm late. Besides, schedules are for suckers.
To-do list:	Gym Ignore desires Please everyone but me Reevaluate my expectations Buy fruits & vegetables	Sleep late Explore desires Please me Raise my expectations Buy banana & cucumber	Sleep late with Jim Indulge desires Feel perfectly pleased being me Raise my rates Buy vibrator
Self-image:	If I were thinner, I'd be better.	If I were thinner, I'd be bitter.	I'm so foxy, I'm attracted to myself!
Attitude:	If I don't get what I want, I don't deserve it.	If I don't get what I want, I haven't tried hard enough.	If I don't get what I want, I deserve something much better.

Worries:	Am I scraping my tongue properly? Do friends read my serious email messages aloud to amuse their coworkers? Am I good enough?	Will anyone notice if I forget to return to work after my three-martini lunch? How many outstanding tickets does it take to get the boot? Am I bad enough?	Will I get fired if I photocopy someone else's butt at the office? Why do I have this job when I could freelance at home naked? Am I going to catch something stealing sips from other people's drinks?
Secret life plan:	If I find a husband I love, I'll never need to work again.	If I find a job I love, I'll never need to find a husband.	If I find my badness, I'll never need anything—but accomplices.
Mantra:	I will survive, I will survive.	I will thrive, I will thrive.	I am queen bee of the hive.
Religious outlook:	Lord help me.	God bless America.	God is a Bad Girl!
Sex life:	I'm too stressed to even think about it.	Is it hot in here? Or could it be global warming?	I'm so hot, I could be causing global warming.
Life's big question:	Why am I alive?	Why have I lived so long without satin sheets?	Why do people leave bed at all when it's such a nice place to entertain?
Today's highlights:	Ate fat-free all day. Saved $1.12 buying TP in bulk. Made amends at work.	Ate for free all day. Saved $6.12 lifting TP from the office. Made a mess at work.	Ate for three all day. TP'd my ex's car and boss's house. Made out work.

how to find your badness

There's a bad girl inside every girl. You may not feel it. You may not believe it. But she's there. Dig up some old photo albums from your childhood. Look at pictures of yourself when you were 10 or 12, seven or eight, four or five. Go back as far as you have to go to find the impish grin, the sparkly eyes, the girl in ridiculous outfits that only she could love and appreciate. Look for the smirk, look for the fire, look for the little girl who didn't know enough to be afraid of her own wants. When you spot her, you'll know it.

Being a bad girl isn't about breaking the law. It's about breaking the rules—and respecting yourself in the morning. **Note to Self:** Indulge early and often.

To-Do List	To-Don't List
be fearless	be a wimp
be passionate	be self-destructive
be a rebel	be a whiner
be an independent thinker	be a bitch
be the anti-Barbie	be a power-tripper
be satisfied	be hard as nails
be yourself	be a felon
	be a phony

cute, confident, and carefree as I was when I was 12.   I want to impact others

Bad Girl Confessions

Bad Girl Confession #1

I really wanted to win the prize for the Easter Egg Hunt, which was a real white bunny rabbit. So I secretly combined my Easter eggs with my brother's eggs. We won, and I had to clean up rabbit shit for the next 10 years.

Bad Girl Confession #2

I'm not very bad yet—but I'm seriously working on it.

Bad Girl Confession #3

I really wanted a Miss Piggy watch for my communion. I was a devoted Miss Piggy fan and I needed this watch! I promised to be good and take care of it and assured my parents that 50 dollars was not too much for my happiness. I got it and boy was it ugly! I threw it out soon after.

Bad Girl Confession #4

I tell people it's decaf when it's not.

Bad Girl Confession #5

My stepmother is this competitive, perfectionist orchid fanatic. I mixed a bunch of salt in with her expensive designer orchid food. Guess what died? Thank God for her Valium.

Bad Girl Icons

Need a strategy for getting what you want—bad girl style? Take a lesson from the pros. A quick review of these legendary bad girls and their unique getting-it styles and you'll

Bad Girl Icons	Do
Eve	Honor your desires and appetite. Challenge authority figures.
Holly Golightly	Look fabulous 24/7. Use an alias and your feminine wiles.
Madonna	Be shamelessly ambitious and work your ass off. Exploit your talents and ignore your weaknesses.
Rosa Parks	Take a stand for what you believe in. Behave with absolute dignity and entitlement.
Lucy Ricardo	Pretend you're totally clueless. Win them over with your wacky humor.
Oprah Winfrey	Show your emotions—and every ounce of personal strength. Become a fearless leader.

and Their Strategies for Getting into the Swirl

be set. At least one of these approaches will work in every situation. Make like Madonna? Pull a Rosa? Do an Oprah? It all depends on you, the situation, and what you want.

Don't	The Result
Be ashamed of your naked body. Be surprised when sparks fly and things start to happen fast.	Keep them interested.
Ever get caught trying. Take any of it too seriously.	Keep them paying.
Doubt yourself for an instant. Be afraid to shock people with your talents or your weaknesses.	Keep them guessing.
Budge, no matter what. Be surprised if you change the world.	Keep them honest.
Let them see how smart you are. Be afraid to make a fool of yourself.	Keep them laughing.
Waste time hiding your vulnerabilities. Be afraid of your own ambition.	Keep them inspired.

Are You a Bad Girl? [A Quiz]

1. The last time I got naked with a stranger I was _____.
A. at the doctor's office
B. in the dressing room at Loehmann's
C. at 35,000 feet

2. How do you spell relief during a stressful work day?
A. R-o-l-a-i-d-s
B. B-o-u-r-b-o-n
C. O-r-g-a-s-m-s

3. Once, I stretched _____ to get what I wanted.
A. my allowance for a whole month
B. the truth about my last job
C. a waistband over my head

4. When I call in sick, I'm usually in bed with _____.
A. a fever over 101
B. a hangover
C. a new friend

5. Hustling men at a bar for free drinks is _____.
A. tacky in a bad way
B. tacky in a good way
C. called Happy Hour

6. When I plan for the future, I think about _____.
A. mutual funds
B. my next relationship
C. mutual fun

7. The last time I got spanked, I _____.
A. was nine and I deserved it
B. lost a bet
C. asked for it

8. When I see myself going down, I'm _____.
A. riding in an elevator
B. at a Nordstrom sale instead of at therapy, again
C. winking at myself in a mirror

9. I _____ to get what I want.
A. am way too embarrassed
B. know exactly what to do
C. exist

10. If anyone at the meeting knew what I was thinking, ____.
A. I'd get a gold star for staying focused
B. they'd call security
C. I'd be fired, sue them hard, and make a million on a made-for-TV movie about my life

11. My sex life is best described by the song _____.
A. "I'd Do Anything for Love (But I Won't Do That)," by Meatloaf
B. "Me in Honey," by R.E.M.
C. "Sex-O-Matic Venus Freak," by Macy Gray

12. I believe the truth _____.
A. shall set you free
B. is open to interpretation, kind of like time
C. is just one of the things that hurts when you drink too much

13. My favorite form of multitasking is _____.
A. faking an orgasm while masturbating
B. having an orgasm while shopping online
C. faking not having an orgasm in spinning class

14. I met my last date while ___.
A. in-line skating in the park
B. on-line dating at the office
C. leading the conga line at a wedding reception I crashed

15. I have no _____ and that's how I like it.
A. strong opinions or desires
B. STDs
C. regrets

Nada Bad Girl

If you answered **A** to most questions, you're so good it hurts—and that's not the point of life! You need to cut loose, cut yourself some slack, cut your hair—do anything to free yourself up for some fun. If you don't find your bad girl self pronto, you may implode. (That can be so messy. And you know how you feel about making a mess.)

Baby Bad Girl

If you answered **B** to most questions, you're borderline bad. Keep up the bad work! Just set your badness goals and keep your eye on the prize—your happiness. Remember, when you play with girls who are badder than you, your game improves much faster!

Diva Bad Girl

If you answered **C** to most questions, you are bad to the bone—and irresistible. Parents fear you, children revere you, pets follow you everywhere, and all of your friends secretly want to be you. Congratulations. You are living in the pearl of the Bad Girl Swirl. Enjoy!

The Bad Girl 'Tude

Most people have this crazy idea that you need some special reason, skill, or power to be confident. Ridiculous.

Can't remember the last time you felt confident? Just strike a pose. Your body will remember and the feeling will spread. The secret ingredient in your bad girl 'tude is confidence.

Note to Self: Check for holes in butt seam of leggings before yoga class.

Diva power   Kick-boxer power

daily, in some meaningful way, but not take it all seriously. I want to be a fashion

Charlie's Angels power

Academy Award–winner power

Talk-show hostess power

designer.   I want a balance of career, love, and friendship.   I want sex daily.

Mother, May I?

No! You don't need your mother's permission—or anyone else's permission—to get what you want. No matter how well your mother thinks she knows you or how often she thinks she is you, what she wants for you is not the same as what you want.

Even if your mother is an annoying Bossy the Cow or acts as if your life is a do-over for hers, you can still learn from her years of experience and repression. Just run her comments through your bad girl filter and you'll hear exactly what you want to hear.

Note to Self: You do not have to grow up and become your mother.

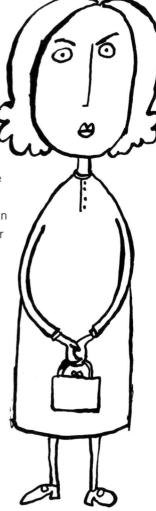

I want to be famous for something revolutionary. I want creative freedom. I want

After Applying the Bad Girl Filter . . .

What Your Mother Says	What You Hear Her Say
I just want what's best for you.	*Be whoever you want to be!*
You should buy more matching outfits.	*I want to take you shopping.*
Pull your hair back to show off your pretty face.	*Cut your hair super short.*
I hope you meet a nice, handsome man who can make you happy.	*Date a lot and find out who does it for you in the sack.*
Wear less black.	*Wear a shorter black skirt.*
He's not good enough for you.	*Polygamy for women is a great idea!*
Put sunscreen on every inch of your body.	*Nude sunbathing is the bomb!*
Tweeze your brows.	*Sneeze at cows.*
Don't ever sit on public toilet seats.	*Pee in the wild whenever you want.*
Are you wearing any underwear?	*Your butt looks terrific!*
I hope you're being careful.	*Have all the fun I never had—just don't get knocked up and don't marry some guy you don't love.*

world peace and great sex.   I want straight hair, straight teeth, and big boobs.   I

Stay Tuned

If you're constantly paying attention to what everyone else wants, it's impossible to get a true read on your own wants.

Tune out . . .

All advertisers

They want your money.

They want you to feel insecure/ugly/fat without them.

They want your email address.

Your parents

They want you to make them look good to their friends.

They want you to be happy, as long as your definition of happiness is the same as theirs.

They want you to do well—but not so well that they feel like losers compared to you.

Your peers

They want you to reinforce them and their worst decisions.

They want you to buy stuff so they can borrow it from you.

They want you to try it first, in case it's really gross or it hurts a lot.

Your inner bitch

She wants to make you miserable with constant criticism.

She wants to fill you with self-doubt.

She wants a drink.

Tune in . . .

Your appetite and your ambition

Your secret desires and your wildest dreams

Your pleasure principle

want to be on Oprah.   I want a well-dressed lover.   I want two well-dressed lovers.

Just Say "No!"

The first step to becoming a real bad girl is learning to say no. You just gotta do it. Learn to say no to your parents (they certainly have said it to you). Say it to your boss, your lover, even to your friends. You can't begin to get what you want if you're busy giving everyone else what they want.

The first few times you say no, you get this crazy little adrenaline rush.

Note to Self: Natural deodorant? No.

If it seems terrifying or impossible to say no to the people in your life, start slowly to practice and build your confidence.

* When the dental hygienist asks if you're having a good day, just say "No." (Even if you are.)
* If a guy at a coffeehouse approaches you and asks if he can share your table, just say "No." (No explanation or apology needed.)

Note to Self: Just say no to guilt, especially when saying no.

No Fear

Do you have the idea that it's unladylike to want? Snap out of it! The second you start ignoring your desires, you're a regular at the snooze bar of life. Don't be afraid to want things, to yearn, crave, or lust for anything. And don't be afraid to go after what you want. If you can't satisfy yourself then how can you expect anyone else to satisfy you?

Note to Self: If you don't follow through on your big ideas, someone else will.

I want to want nothing. I want a huge, beautiful bathroom with a fabulous view.

How Do You Get

Enter key words on eBay. *(Cate, age 30)*

Flirt, flirt, and then flirt some more.
  (Suzanne, age 22)

I bleach my hair platinum. Everything else follows.
  (Christy, age 29)

Flatter, charm, demand, push, threaten (in that order).
  (Cynthia, age 29)

Pretend I don't really want it. *(Jordan, age 37)*

I pray. I cry. I stomp my feet. I yell. I beg. I plead. I buy
  shoes. *(Mary, age 34)*

I pretty much just take it. *(Patti, age 42)*

Slowly. *(Julie, age 33)*

Get naked. (Not recommended in job interviews.)
  (Gretchen, age 31)

I ask for it. *(Kim, age 24)*

Do unto others so they will do unto me.
  (Terri, age 53)

First I affect disinterest, then I construct compelling,
tautology-strewn, verbiage-filled, Jesuitical arguments in
my favor, and I finish with tears. If necessary, I will
repeat from affected disinterest.
  (Jenn, age 27)

Worry. *(Jane, age 21)*

Knee-high black suede boots with a really short skirt.
  (Lisa, age 29)

What You Want?

Work hard and act fairly straightforward, actually.
(Samantha, age 30)

Pretend to be blind. I've gotten really good at it.
(Cameron, age 34)

Be as charming as possible while withholding.
(Patty, age 38)

Use humor, have compassion, and if that fails, a thick
stack of 20s. *(Halle, age 35)*

I don't know. Next question, please. *(Maya, age 26)*

By not taking life personally. *(Maria, age 32)*

Play rock, scissors, paper. (Rock wins 93% of the time.)
(Amy, age 28)

Pray. *(Kathleen, age 31)*

The hair flip and attitude get me in the door and brains
get me the sale. If I think the sale might collapse, I rely
on my Ultra Brite smile and knowledge of the Chicago
Bears defensive line. Make no mistake, these traits are
not mutually exclusive.
(Lisa, age 28)

The yellow pages. *(Susan, age 26)*

Admitting what I want and figuring out a plan to get it.
Feng shui helps too. *(Karla, age 37)*

I keep asking for it over and over again until whoever is
responsible breaks down and gives it to me.
(Alicia, age 27)

Trust Your Body

Not sure if you really want it? Just fill out the following checklist. Your mind plays tricks on you, but your body never lies—even when you wish it would.

When I think about it . . .

- ☐ I can't sleep
- ☐ I can't eat
- ☐ My palms sweat
- ☐ Something else sweats
- ☐ I get goose bumps
- ☐ The back of my neck tingles
- ☐ My mouth gets dry
- ☐ My heart races
- ☐ My teeth hurt
- ☐ I blush
- ☐ I feel dizzy
- ☐ The heavy breathing starts
- ☐ I get so excited I have to pee

If you checked one, it could be a fluke. If you checked two or more, you want it and you want it bad. So you better devise a plan of action for getting it.

I want to order a minibike through the mail.   I want fashion to be divinely

The Road to Satisfaction

inspired–and affordable. I want a family. I want more credit, more clothes, and

Are You Really as

Maybe you only think you're getting everything you want. If you're having one of these **anxiety dreams** (or any others), then you're definitely not getting enough of what you want—or what you really want at all. Maybe

- [ ] All your teeth fall out.
- [ ] You're falling off a cliff.
- [ ] You're drowning.
- [ ] You're trying to run away and you can't move.
- [ ] You're starring in a show and don't know any of your lines.
- [ ] You're riding the bus naked.
- [ ] You're at school naked.
- [ ] You're at work naked.
- [ ] You're giving a speech naked.
- [ ] You're having a baby.
- [ ] You're having someone else's baby.
- [ ] You can't remember if you have a baby or where you left it.
- [ ] You have your baby but it's a Jack Russell terrier.

Satisfied as You Think?

you need more sleep, more fun, more relaxation, or more clothes. Whatever your source of stress, once you find your badness, you'll start sleeping like a baby.

- [ ] You're giving a speech, naked, and all your teeth fall out.
- [ ] You're on *David Letterman* and when you try to talk, your teeth fall out.
- [ ] You're on *David Letterman* and when you try to talk, you realize you're naked.
- [ ] You're on *David Letterman* and when you try to talk, you realize you're naked and Dave is, too.
- [ ] You're walking down the aisle and the groom is nowhere in sight.
- [ ] You're walking down the aisle and you don't know the groom.
- [ ] You're walking down the aisle and you're naked.
- [ ] You're walking down the aisle and all your friends and family are naked.
- [ ] You're walking down the aisle and you realize you're wearing a Hawaiian muumuu.
- [ ] It's second semester of senior year, you haven't done any of the reading or gone to any classes, and you're taking the final exam, naked.

Plagued Personas

If you've become one of these living nightmares, you're not loving life, you're loathing it. Wake up! It's time to open that stress valve in your brain and release your bad girl.

Hardly Any Body

The look: Totally fit.

The attitude: I'm totally fat.

For fun: Exercise, diet, and look in the mirror.

Best quality: Cheap dinner date.

Worst quality: Cheap self-image.

I Dream I'm Jeannie

The look: Soft flesh, soft fabrics.

The attitude: Perky yet helpless.

For fun: Blink, nod, and hope everything will work out.

Best quality: Your belly button.

Worst quality: Calling your man "Master."

Stressy-Bessy

The look: Perfectly crazed and confused.

The attitude: Had one scheduled.

Had to cancel.

For fun: Worry.

Best quality: Never have to diet.

Worst quality: Never have time for your friends.

Dorothy Puker

The look: Urbane and chic.

The attitude: Razor sharp.

For fun: Go out every night and get totally trashed.

Best quality: Extremely funny, clever, and insightful.

Worst quality: You can't remember anything you say or do.

Immaterial Girl

The look: Frumpy and forgettable.

The attitude: Oh, don't mind me.

For fun: Tag along with the few friends you still have.

Best quality: n/a

Worst quality: See above.

I Vanta Trump

The look: High cheekbones, high heels, high maintenance.

The attitude: Caffeinated with artificial sweetener.

For fun: Hunt for a rich man who'll save you.

Best quality: Perfect hair and makeup.

Worst quality: Perfect hair and makeup.

Shoppa Holique

The look: Frantic yet fashionable.

The attitude: Guilty pleasure is the only pleasure.

For fun: Return items you've already worn.

Best quality: Your credit line.

Worst quality: Your credit rating.

Moanica Lewdinsky

The look: Open smile, open legs.

The attitude: Instant gratification, delayed mortification.

For fun: Flash your thong.

Best quality: No gag reflex.

Worst quality: Gag everyone else.

Getting Off the Hook

Problem: named designated driver
Solution: Before you leave the house, gargle with scotch, tequila, or other stinky booze. Dab a splash behind each ear like fine perfume. When you arrive, pretend you're drunk. Greet everyone with a hug, a sloppy kiss, and an "I love you guys!" If that doesn't set you free, weave from lane to lane as you drive to the party or bar and retell the same story over and over again.

Problem: getting coffee for your boss
Solution: If he/she asks for decaf, fetch regular coffee. If he/she asks for regular, fetch decaf. Your boss will either fall asleep or have a mild heart attack. Either way, you're off the hook!

Problem: visible panty lines
Solution: Wear invisible panties.

Problem: a nasty hangover
Solution: Option A: Don't drink too much (boring but effective).

Option B: Drink one glass of water in between every alcoholic drink. Pop a couple of Advil. Sleep late.

Option C: Keep drinking steadily and stay drunk for the rest of your life.

Note to Self: Do not spend your last 10 dollars on lottery tickets and vodka.

a convertible. I want less credit and more sleep. I want a sense of calm, satis-

Problem: stuck taking the notes at all meetings
Solution: Write them up like a bad romance novel. (We had just covered the agenda when Helen arrived late, her full bosom rising and falling with every breath. Loose strands of raven-black hair fell across her cheek and delicate, dewy beads clung above her quivering lip. She quickly found a seat and glanced around the room. When she spied the new client, their eyes locked. He smiled warmly while azure flames illuminated his hard, penetrating stare. They nodded curtly, never hinting at the business they would come to share.)

Problem: busted wearing holey underwear or a padded bra
Solution: Know when to hold it, know when to fold it.

Problem: saggy boobs
Solution: Stand on your head. Secure boobs with duct tape.

Problem: buyer's remorse
Solution: Don't shop with friends who are richer than you. Don't buy anything you don't absolutely love. Don't shop while drunk or stoned.

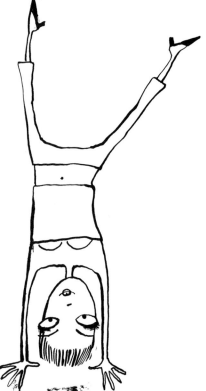

41

faction, and a best-seller. I want true, lasting love. I want the lead in the high

42

school musical. I want a house in the country with an artist's studio. I want

Getting a Date

A date can be a lot of things. An adventure, a night-mare, bad news, good material, a beauty pageant, a boredom buffet, a freak show, a horror show, a game show, a no-show, a spark of hope, too much hype, a nice try, or a nice guy. It can be a new lesson in losers or a new lease on life. But first and foremost, a date is optional. Who you date, how you date, or if you date at all is up to you.

Note to Self: If it's not great sex and it's not true love, it's not worth your time.

Most people take dating way too seriously—and bad girls know better. A bad girl knows that a date should be as simple and carefree as a road trip. All you need to know is what time you're leaving and who you're going with. Beyond that—how you'll pass the time, who you'll meet along the way, or which alias you'll use—is one big mystery. So why worry? If you're constantly imagining what's around the next bend, you're missing the view and the whole point of the ride.

Note to Self: Love? Lust? Can't be sure, better do him again.

Barbie's hair to grow back. I want not to get married in a VFW hall. I want to get

whatever you do,
have fun doing it

Sometimes dating seems like *Mission: Impossible*. We plot, we scheme, we lay traps, we spy, we send our friends out on reconnaissance missions, we do drive-bys, fly-bys, cry-bys. We make crazy late-night phone calls and hang up before saying a word. We act like we can't go on unless we're dating or in a relationship. And when we do go out on dates, the action happens fast. During the first course, we're wondering if he's good in bed. Over the entrée, we're checking our pulse for—could it be?—all the signs of falling in love! By dessert, we're imagining what our kids would look like. On a typical date, we're so out of the moment that we're out of our minds.

If you want to enjoy dating, you have to see it for what it is—a ridiculous sport like badminton or bowling. In fact, dating is a lot like bowling: you can do it in twos or fours or more, you're supposed to keep score, most people look kind of funny doing it, you get to play the angles and grip a lot of different balls, and if you don't pay attention, you'll end up in the gutter. If you take your dating any more seriously than your bowling, you run the risk of becoming a professional dater or, worse yet, ending up in a Friday-night dating league for the rest of your life.

The most important thing to remember is to avoid playing by the rules.

through college. I want a man I could be happy with. I want to be happy with

Popular Forms of Alternative Dating

Does the idea of dating make you jittery? When you picture yourself as a dating diva, do you see a gawky string bean with braces or someone's tired, frumpy, lumpy mother? No problem. You just need to ease into a new way of thinking. Make an attitude adjustment and discover the untapped potential of alternative dating!

* **Dating your pet** (A Chia pet is even less maintenance than a live one.)

* **Dating your bartender** (Ordering a drink is intimate conversation, right?)

* **Dating your job** (Just don't try anything funny with your stapler.)

* **Dating your roommate** (Go ahead and do it—but don't forget it's a bad idea.)

* **Dating your ex-roommate's new roommate** (Be sure to write it all down and sell as a made-for-TV movie later.)

* **Fantasy dating** (Movie stars, musicians, your shrink—dates can even take place on Fantasy Island!)

* **Dating the Internet** (Digital cameras make this option more fun.)

* **Dating a Newfoundlander** (Friends and relatives never get to meet him or know if he really exists.)

* **Dating yourself** (Best of all!)

myself. I want a pony. I want the ability to forgive and rise to the next occasion.

Dating Yourself

Dating yourself is quite possibly the most satisfying way to date. You know from the start that you're building a relationship that will last. You don't have to worry about infidelity. You always get to choose the restaurant and you never have to pretend you're in the mood to see *Baywatch* or anything else. You win every argument, and you'll never lie awake in the wet spot feeling unsatisfied.

How to Date Yourself with Style and Sensitivity

* Eat over the sink by candlelight.

* Surprise yourself with unexpected gifts— a bottle of great champagne, a red rose beside the bed, an X-rated video.

* Treat yourself to a sexy new outfit.

* When you catch your reflection in a store window, flirt shamelessly.

* Buy yourself flowers every week.

* Plan fun weekend getaways to romantic spots.

* Turn the music up and the lights down and slow-dance barefoot in the kitchen.

* Gently caress your hand or your thigh at the movies.

* Sleep in your slinkiest nightgown or nothing at all.

* Whisper sweet nothings into the air, then spin around really fast to catch them in your ear.

* Take long walks in the moonlight, hand in hand, making plans for the future.

Note to Self: Dreaming about babies doesn't mean you want one. Maybe you're dating one?

Note to Self: When having a sexual fantasy in public, try to remember you're in public.

I want to spend a little time in Barbara Eden's bottle. I want safety. I want

When dating yourself, it's important to communicate clearly, just as in any other relationship. Make time for pillow talk a few nights a week. If you set an appointment with yourself, you'll know you have a sacred and safe place where you and your hand mirror can spend some quality time together in bed. Make a ritual of it: turn on soft romantic music, light a candle, and then speak from the heart to your own reflection. "I love spending time with you. You're the best thing that's ever happened to me. It's fun getting to know you. You make me so happy. I've never loved like this before. You complete me." When you say the words out loud, your feelings resonate and actually become more real.

After you've dated yourself for a few months, you'll feel rejuvenated and ready to date other people. Or you may feel rejuvenated and realize you've found your soul mate, the love of your life, and you never want to date anyone else ever again. But either way, you'll feel rejuvenated.

anonymity. I want a maid. I want nurturing. I want shoes with non-slip soles

The Truth about Jobs and Men

What the job really says about the man.

Investment Banker	I look better in my double-breasted suit than I do in my birthday suit, but I'm rich so I hope you won't notice.
Producer	I'm charming with little substance—and a little substance-abuse problem.
Postal Worker	I'm really lazy or kind of crazy—but probably both!
E-Commerce Executive	I have no idea what I'm doing, but I could be a millionaire before anyone finds out.
Editor	I have a half-finished novel in my computer—and always will.
Special Ed. Teacher	I'm above materialism—and by the way, I drive a Dodge Dart.
Entrepreneur	I'm always looking for my next hot girl . . . er, deal.
Artist	I come from money. I run from money.

Lawyer	We will argue, I will win, and you will pay for it.
Actor	I didn't get enough attention as a child, but I did get lots of orthodontia.
Stand-up Comedian	I didn't get enough attention as a child, and I didn't get any orthodontia.
High School Teacher	I didn't make it as a stand-up comedian.
Graphic Designer	Can we pretend I'm an artist?
Writer	I'm memorizing every clever, insightful thing you say. Of course, I'll change your name and take all the credit when I use it.
Freelancer	I have commitment issues.
Career Counselor	I couldn't find mine.
Computer Programmer	My best social skill is typing.
Highway Patrol Officer	I'm a top.

the dating pool

When you're feeling so hot you could pop Jiffy Pop on your butt, then you're ready to dive back into the dating pool—that virtual ocean of splashy shindigs, socialized health clubs, and shark-infested watering holes. You're a bad girl on a big-game hunt and it's survival of the fittest. But have no fear—your bad girl is here.

When introducing yourself in the dating pool, don't use your plain old everyday name—add a sexy little prefix. Alliteration is always a smart choice. It not only serves as a mnemonic device to help new friends remember your name, it also plants an image in their mind that will spark meaningful conversation.

"Hello, I'm . . . Delectable Donna."

Or better yet, don't use your name at all—use an alias.

The Beauty of a Bad Girl Alias

An alias is your quick-release tool to get out of your everyday rut and into your bad girl groove in seconds. Choose an alias that makes you feel super bad. It can be silly, sassy, flashy, sexy, exotic, or whatever gives you the freedom to bust loose, the confidence to break your own rules, and the cover you need when making a quick get-away. If you're facing a bad girl block, use the instant alias finder.

that are also sexy.   I want inspiring, loving friends.   I want a swimming pool.

Instant Alias Finder

	First Name	Last Name	Examples
Your Dating Diva name	something sweet within sight	any liquid in your kitchen	*Honey Bourbon* *Pop-Tart Tonic* *Cinnamon Cream*
Your Girl Detective name	favorite baby animal	where you last went to school	*Chick Providence* *Kitten San Diego* *Gosling Chicago*
Your Barfly name	the last snack food you ate	your favorite drink	*Twinkie Cosmo* *Snickers Manhattan* *Cheetos Martini*

I want work that makes me feel like a big shot and is fun and sounds cool at

How to Increase Your Sex Appeal

An alias is a good place to start—but you have to follow up with attitude! No one else will think you're sexy unless you do. So do whatever it takes to live the bad girl dream. Put yourself in clothing, situations, and positions that raise your baddy temperature.

* Dance in the nude with the shades up.
* Record your answering machine message while masturbating. (Whenever you doubt your sex appeal, just call home!)
* Tidy up around the house in nothing but black stockings and stiletto heels.
* Wear black leather pants to the grocery store, to church, to bed.
* Buy a vibrator and use it.
* Read erotic fiction in public places.

Note to Self: Visit barbershop. Think about it. All guys—no competition!

cocktail parties. I want a lover who makes me feel like both Elvis and Priscilla. I

Dating Pool Rules

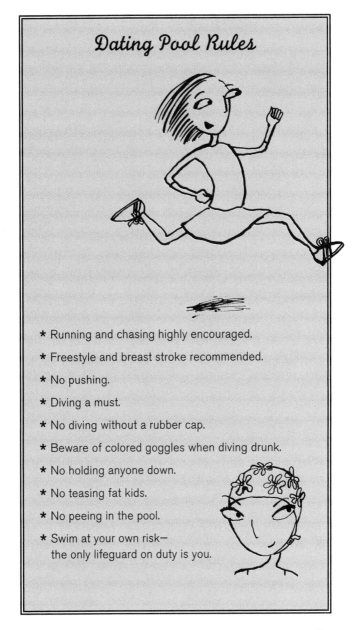

* Running and chasing highly encouraged.

* Freestyle and breast stroke recommended.

* No pushing.

* Diving a must.

* No diving without a rubber cap.

* Beware of colored goggles when diving drunk.

* No holding anyone down.

* No teasing fat kids.

* No peeing in the pool.

* Swim at your own risk—
  the only lifeguard on duty is you.

want to be butch. I want to be perfect. I want a 1975 white Mercedes sedan.

Sexy Power Poses

Want to find your inner sex kitten and transform her into a wild animal? Of course you do! Just lower the lights to the most flattering level (so low you can't see a single flaw but bright enough that you can still see it's you). Then stretch out in front of a full-length mirror with a Victoria's Secret catalog and (no, not that!) practice these sexy power poses.

The Power Pout
* Bite and pinch your lips until slightly swollen
* Grease lips with glossy lipstick or other shiny lubricant
* Open lips just wide enough to hold a lipstick

The Urban Sprawl
* Tousle hair
* Stretch out on bed or bearskin rug
* Throw one arm over head
* Arch back to elevate boobs until you're in pain

Baddy Bedroom Eyes
* Apply massive amounts of eye makeup
* Tousle hair
* Lower eyelids to half mast

The Seductive Armpit Sniff
* Pull back hair with both hands
* Gently arch lower back
* Drop head seductively
* Part lips and sniff armpit

Stepped in Something Saucy
* Tousle hair
* Wear black stockings and stiletto heels
* Stick out butt
* Lift one heel to check for drippings

Quick-draw McBra
* Tousle hair
* Take a wide stance
* Cock hip to one side
* Tuck shootin' hand into undies above opposite hip

Note to Self: Drink shot of whiskey before next bikini wax.

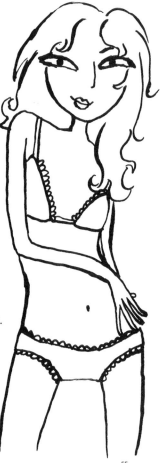

ple and a down comforter. I want a yellow cottage in San Francisco with a

The Man Translator

It's tempting to think all your problems will go away once you start dating and get into a relationship. But the truth is, your old problems don't go away—you get new ones! When it comes to tackling a communication gap, remember that knowledge is power. As long as you read between the lines, you'll stay in the driver's seat.

What He Says	What He Means
I really get into talking about my feelings.	I'll talk about feelings if it gets me into your pants.
I'm not very close to my family.	Will you be my mommy?
Ikea rocks!	I've got huge student loans.
I go out with my buddies at least once a week.	I'm dating other women.
I love lingerie!	Can I try on yours?
I talk to my parents every day.	Are you codependent too?
I'm not looking for a serious relationship right now.	Wanna do it?

I don't believe in sex before marriage.

I'd love for you to meet my mother on our second date.

I still really value you as a friend.

My career has always been my top priority.

The sexiest thing about you is your mind.

I work out a lot.

This is so special. Let's keep it between us.

She has nothing to do with us.

My pager is the best way to reach me.

I think we should slow things down for a while.

I think I'm gay, but humor me for a few months, okay?

I'm definitely gay, but cover for me for a few months, okay?

I still want you for booty calls.

I have a two-inch penis.

You're not that attractive but I'll still sleep with you.

I really love my body! Can I show you?

I'd be totally humiliated if anyone knew we were dating.

I don't even think about you when I sleep with her.

I'm married.

Oh, shit. I'm falling in love.

The Perfect Blind Date

If you're not meeting the right kinds of people, you may be stuck in a kiddie-size dating pool—and every bad girl deserves an Olympic array of lanes and choices. A blind date can be your diving board to the deep end.

The perfect blind date is short—not in stature but in length. Ten minutes is all you need to know if you want to see him again or run for it. Why risk ruining an entire evening with a loser when you can end the pain in 10 minutes? Whether you're meeting people online, through the personals, or via your aunt Edna's best friend's nephew's roommate, be sure to set it up as a 10-minute date in advance so he knows what to expect. If he's ever suffered through a nightmare blind date before (and who hasn't), he'll be relieved to know you're a shrewd operator.

The 10-minute Date

Arrange to meet at a public place, ideally a popular bar or café. (Make sure a friend or coworker knows your plan and the guy's name, just in case.)

- Use an alias—just for kicks.
- Order one drink.
- Ask him only three questions:

> What's your favorite movie?
> Where do you buy your shoes?
> How do you define foreplay?

- While listening to his answers, ask yourself three questions:

> Do I want to kiss this guy?
> Do I want to wake up naked next to this guy?
> Do I want to have this guy's children?

- Look him up and down.
- Judge him all around.

If you like what you see and hear, take his phone number. (Do not give him yours, yet.) If you don't like what you see or hear, shake his hand and thank him for his time, or just give him a fake phone number. It's that easy!
• Get out of there.

For maximum efficiency, set up three or four of these 10-minute dates for the same evening. You only have to dress and beauty-up once, and it's much easier to compare and contrast when the options are fresh in your mind—like your own private *Dating Game.*

Note to Self: Buy more microcassettes for hidden tape recorder.

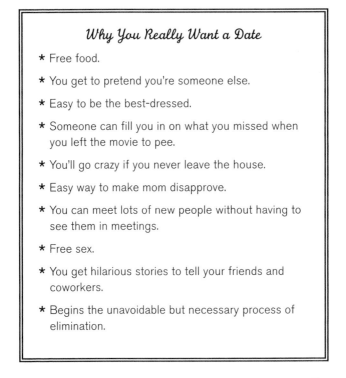

Why You Really Want a Date

★ Free food.

★ You get to pretend you're someone else.

★ Easy to be the best-dressed.

★ Someone can fill you in on what you missed when you left the movie to pee.

★ You'll go crazy if you never leave the house.

★ Easy way to make mom disapprove.

★ You can meet lots of new people without having to see them in meetings.

★ Free sex.

★ You get hilarious stories to tell your friends and coworkers.

★ Begins the unavoidable but necessary process of elimination.

companions.   I want firm breasts and a tall boyfriend.   I want a baby.   I want a

Girl's Guide to Hunting and Kissing

Humans have evolved from hunter-gatherers into hunter-sample-ers. Before we commit, we try on, we road-test, we taste-test, we compare prices, features, sizes, and colors. We sample everything in advance but what matters most—kisses. A bad girl knows it's her right and privilege to sample, taste-test, and compare kisses before committing to a date. A great kiss can last all night but a bad kiss can last a lifetime.

If you see something you think you want while out on a social safari, you should kiss it to know for sure. When hunting and kissing, it's very important to look your best, taste your best, and kiss your best.

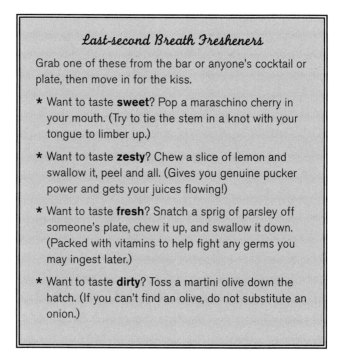

Last-second Breath Fresheners

Grab one of these from the bar or anyone's cocktail or plate, then move in for the kiss.

* Want to taste **sweet**? Pop a maraschino cherry in your mouth. (Try to tie the stem in a knot with your tongue to limber up.)

* Want to taste **zesty**? Chew a slice of lemon and swallow it, peel and all. (Gives you genuine pucker power and gets your juices flowing!)

* Want to taste **fresh**? Snatch a sprig of parsley off someone's plate, chew it up, and swallow it down. (Packed with vitamins to help fight any germs you may ingest later.)

* Want to taste **dirty**? Toss a martini olive down the hatch. (If you can't find an olive, do not substitute an onion.)

trip to Japan. I want enlightenment. I want to be the favorite child. I want a has-

Direct Hit

Plant your feet in a wide, sexy stance, cock your hip, extend one arm, and point your finger provocatively at the wild beast of your choice. Then in a clear, loud, seductive, crowd-pleasing voice, say, "I want you! I want you! You! You! You!" When all eyes are on you, do your best Tina Turner, diva-bad-girl strut across the room and plant a big wet one on his lips. With the crowd cheering you on, no self-respecting man will deny you.

Note to Self: Do not schedule a facial before a date, unless you want him to ask you if you were stung by wasps.

Boogie Lips

It's just like asking someone to dance. Seductively dance your way over to the partner of your dreams, lean in close, and whisper, "I love this song. Wanna kiss?" If the setting is a bit more formal, you may want to extend your hand, introduce yourself, then say, "May I have the next kiss?" Works best if music is actually playing.

Note to Self: Relationship red flags are not green for a reason.

The Grab Student

A perfect choice when you're dressed down or can't afford to buy your next drink. Pull out a pen and paper or a lip liner and cocktail napkin, then casually approach your research assistant. Say something like this: "Excuse, me. I'm doing research for my master's thesis on the evolution of courtship and copulation in the 21st century. I was wondering if I could ask you one question." When he says yes, say, "Can I kiss

sle-free, independent, creative, part-time career. I want ultimate freedom of

you? I'm developing my super-kiss theory and I'd love to study your technique." Afterward, be sure to thank him and jot down a few quick notes.

Mack Attack

Sometimes the best approach is the strong, silent type. Swish on over to your Mack Daddy, grab him by the tie, the lapels, or the back of the head, and mack him good! Don't let him up for air until he submits to a little tongue lashing. Then just walk off without a word, swinging your hips with every step. Avoid macking guys who are out with other women, unless you want to get slapped—which actually can be very thrilling and a great way to get some tender lovin' care from other men. Just be prepared.

choice. **I want all the joys of children with none of the heavy strings. I want**

Bad Girl Confessions ✌

Bad Girl Confession #6

I was flying business class and masturbated—very successfully—with no hands while pretending to read the *Wall Street Journal*. It's still my favorite form of in-flight entertainment.

Bad Girl Confession #7

I kept a key to my boyfriend's van after we broke up. Whenever I see it parked somewhere, I pee in it.

Bad Girl Confession #8

I had a quickie in the Ladies' Powder Room at the Waldorf Astoria. Of course, I tipped the attendant quite well.

Bad Girl Confession #9

I backed into a meter maid on purpose.

Bad Girl Confession #10

I snuck into a college date party in disguise (blond wig, sunglasses, huge fake boobs) to see who my old boyfriend had taken to the party instead of me. She was nothing. And I got asked out by one of his fraternity brothers. I declined—I didn't want to wear the fake boobs ever again.

bad girl bar talk

Want to turn heads when you walk into a bar? Just order one of these bad girl drinks in a loud, clear voice with a devilish smile on your face. Be sure you know the ingredients, in case the bartender is stumped or scared stiff. It kind of ruins the moment if you haven't a clue what goes into your badass beverage. Here are some favorite head-turners, guaranteed to get a reaction from the crowd—and an evening of free drinks.

"Hey, Bartender!" (Say it loud and proud):

I'd like a strong **Piece of Ass**.

I feel like an **Axe Murderer** tonight.

I'm really craving a **Bad Habit** tonight.

Get me an **Absolutely Screwed Up**.

I'm definitely craving an **Affair**.

I need a **Big Unit** pronto.

I feel like a **Dirty Girl Scout** tonight.

I'm in the mood for a **Ménage à Trois**.

This girl needs a **Lube Job** bad tonight.

I'd like a **Wet Kiss**, please.

Can you give me a **Screaming Orgasm**?

If not, I'll take a **Vibrator**.

I need a pitcher of **Pure Ecstasy**.

But I'll settle for a **Horny Bull**.

I think I'll take a **Lesbian Lover** tonight.

Aretha Franklin's attitude and her "tell you off" voice. I want fame for my unique

A real bad girl calls her own shots and calls her own drink. "Hey bartender, make me a **Bad Girl!**"

A Bad Girl cocktail is sophisticated, sexy, and complex—just like you. It looks kind of sweet and innocent, but it's really strong and packs an irresistible punch.

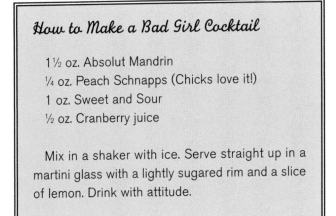

How to Make a Bad Girl Cocktail

1 ½ oz. Absolut Mandrin
¼ oz. Peach Schnapps (Chicks love it!)
1 oz. Sweet and Sour
½ oz. Cranberry juice

Mix in a shaker with ice. Serve straight up in a martini glass with a lightly sugared rim and a slice of lemon. Drink with attitude.

Once you find your badness, you'll attract males like a dog in heat. They won't be able to help themselves when they see your confidence and command of the bartender's handbook. To get a quick read on the pack, go right to the top; take a look at a man's hair and you'll know whether to head him off at or before the pass.

Note to Self: If planning to undress for an audience, wear matching bra and underwear or nothing at all.

opinion and creations. I want to take my baby on a trip around the world in a

The Truth about Hair and Men

Here's what the hair really says about the man.

Style	What He Thinks It Says	What It Really Says
Shaved head	I'm a really bad dude.	I'm a really bald dude.
Toupee	Hey, baby, I'm still a stud.	At least I can afford fake hair.
Comb-over	Look, I've still got hair!	Look! It's the emperor's new hair!
Full beard	I am a rugged, fearless guy.	I miss Grizzly Adams.

Big mustache	I play pro baseball.	Burt Reynolds is my hero.
Crew cut	I'm a real macho man.	I'm so confused.
Soul patch	I'm way cool.	I was a total dork in high school.
Goatee	I'm a creative intellectual.	I'm stuck in the '90s.
Dreadlocks	I'm getting back to my roots.	I've got stinky roots.
Mullet	My hair is cutting-edge hip.	My hair is heinous.
Slicked back	I'm a serious power broker.	No one ever takes me seriously.

How to Score More Free Drinks

You can't get your bad girl merit badge without knowing how to score free drinks in any bar on any night of the week. Don't think of it as scamming or getting something for nothing. Think of it as giving something back to mankind. Yes, you're giving the gift of chivalry, creating an opportunity for some kind person to help another less fortunate human being and, in return, feel bigger and better about himself. It's a nice little ego booster. Most men not only love it—they need it.

When you're on the scam, you attract a lot more freebies with honey than you do with vinegar. So be sweet, be sexy, be charming. Then everyone wins, and no one gets hurt. A little kindness and a lot of flattery goes a long way between strangers. Try these top-shelf techniques developed by the pros, or be spontaneous and invent your own.

Silly (Exotic) Me!

Order your drink as usual, then act completely surprised and quite flustered when you open your wallet and find nothing but foreign currency. Then act really embarrassed and apologetic and loudly sputter something like, "Silly me! I've been so busy unpacking I've forgotten to change my lire/francs/yen/NYC subway tokens." Then gaze around the bar like a doe until some gallant soul offers to pay for your drink. Be prepared to chat him or her up with your exciting tales from abroad. If you're a skilled raconteur, you'll be drinking free for the rest of the night.

backpack.   I want to eliminate all the really useless people from all places I go or

I'm Such a Klutz!

The accidental elbow bump is the perfect tactic when drinking a martini, cosmopolitan, or other precariously packaged semiprecious cocktail. Plus, many men mistake klutziness for sexiness. If you're drinking a cocktail with color, down about half of your drink, then surreptitiously fill it back up with water. (Take a mouthful from your water glass and slyly transfer it into your cocktail glass while pretending to take a sip.) If your cocktail is clear, you can down the whole thing and just refill it with water. Be sure to leave the olive or onion untouched so the drink will look brand new.

Bump One: Find a respectable-looking guy in a business suit or crisp pressed Wranglers leaning with his elbow on the bar. Casually place your glass on the edge of the bar about an inch away from his elbow. Then start fishing for something in your purse until your drink goes flying. Extra points if your drink spills all over you. Best in crowded bars.

Bump Two: Spot a group of animated guys. Target the loud-mouthed, wildly gesticulating guy telling the stories. If he's holding a drink, see which hand it's in. Then slowly walk by him on the side opposite his drink, holding your drink out in front of you. With any luck, he'll throw out his

live. I want a 10 million-dollar bank account so I don't have to answer to anyone.

free arm or step backward enough to jostle you. Of course, he doesn't have to actually touch you for your drink to go flying. You could just be reacting to his sudden movement. If any of the guys in his group see your drink spill, he'll be shamed into buying you another one. Best in crowded bars.

Bump Three: Ask the bartender for a menu or something else that he has to hand to you. When you reach out for it, knock over your drink with the outside of your elbow. The bartender will not only see the spill, he'll also feel partly responsible. Any respectable bartender will offer to replace your cocktail on the spot. Works under any conditions.

Secret Agent Stealth Sipper

Grab a few of those long, narrow, red bar straws. If you can't find the long ones, build your own by pinching the end of one and sticking it inside another until you've got a two-foot-long lethal weapon. Then casually work the room, stealing sips from other people's drinks. With a friend, you can trade off creating a distraction for each other or turn it into a competition. (Whoever gets bombed first wins!) Best in dark, crowded bars.

I want better sex. I want my brother to go somewhere for a very long time. I want

Men behind Bars

Always keep in mind that the bartender is your friend. He's the go-to guy and the man with the power. So treat him with respect, learn his name, or call him darlin', handsome, or cupcake. And flirt with him—no matter how old he is or what he looks like. If he's not too busy, ask him about himself. If he's slammed, just make eye contact and give him a big, wet smile from time to time. Unless the bartender actually owns the joint (which is highly unlikely), he won't care how many times he pours you another drink as long as you're improving his view and the quality of his life behind the bar. If the bartender is a woman, 99 percent of the same rules apply—everyone likes to be liked.

Sometimes a direct one-liner is the best approach when you want to keep the drinks flowing freely.

Hey, Bartender . . . !

"I'm not feeling a thing. Can you add a splash?"

"There's a bug in my drink!"

"There's a hair in my drink!"

"Someone just sneezed in my drink!"

"Some guy just drank half my drink!"

"Handsome, would you be real sweet and top this off for me?"

to play kickball and go sledding way past dark. I want to be a beautician. I want

Seductive Secrets

Know what you want and how to get it.

I Want to Get Lucky

If you own anything that remotely resembles a wedding band or engagement ring, wear it on your ring finger to a bar or club. Find an object of your desire, talk him up, look him down, flirt him all around. Eventually, he will notice that you're wearing a ring. When he asks if you're married, slowly and seductively run your tongue around your ring finger, pull off the ring, and say in your baddest bedroom voice, "I'm not married tonight."

He'll want you even more if he thinks you're married and willing to risk it all for one night of hot sex with him. Technically, you're just telling the truth. So what's the big deal if he finds out that you're not married any night? And if he ends up grossing you out later in the evening, you have the perfect exit strategy.

Note to Self: Never, ever catch the bouquet at your ex's wedding, even if it hits you in the face.

I Want to Go Home with the Cute Guy

Only go out to parties and bars with friends who are uglier than you.

some sexy, slobbering, partying boyfriend. I want to throw great parties with pop-

I Want Him to Call

When the guy you've been talking up at a party or bar asks for your number and you want him to call you, write it on his stomach in lipstick. He'll definitely

remember you. You also can check out what kind of shape he's in. And if he goes home with another woman later that night, you can be sure he won't be getting any.

I Want Great, No-Strings-Attached, Casual Sex

Only sleep with promiscuous people. It's counterintuitive but smart. Think about it—people who sleep around have a lot to offer. (Just don't forget the body condom.)
* They're really good at sex. (Practice makes perfect!)
* They can keep it light and fun in bed.
* They know how to avoid getting emotionally entangled.
* They don't care whether or not you're marriage material.

Note to Self: Do not do a politician under any circumstances.

I Want to Feel Naughty

During dinner, secretly slip out of your panties without your date noticing. (This takes real skill and may require some subtle pelvic thrusts, which should keep dinner quite interesting—at least for you. Slide out of one shoe, then the other. If another restaurant patron catches your action, just smile devilishly at him and wink.) When you've completely removed your panties, hold them tightly in one hand, and excuse yourself for the ladies' room. As

73

you pass by your date, lean over, give him a little peck on the cheek, and slip your panties into his jacket pocket. You've set up a win-win situation for yourself when he finds them later in the evening. If you're into him, it's a total turn-on. If you're not into him, act thoroughly disgusted when he pulls a strange pair of women's panties out of his pocket and insist that he take you home immediately. (For best results, make sure you're wearing black lacy panties—not your tighty-whities.)

I Want to Feel Wanted

Get really drunk, write lewd, suggestive postcards, and mail them to yourself at home and at your office. When you get them, you won't even remember that you wrote them yourself!

Recommended messages:

"Thinking of you—naked in front of the fire."

"I can't get you out of my dirty little head."

I want longer orgasms.   I want one sweet, loving man and one baby.   I want to

"I want to spank you with a wet hand."

"Without you, I'm nothing!"

Be sure to disguise your handwriting so that you, your coworkers, and your roommates won't know you wrote them.

I Want to Meet Big, Strong Guys Who Know How to Cook

Set off fire alarms and wait around for the firemen to arrive.

I Want to Keep My Man

Sometimes you have to treat him mean to keep him keen. Withhold oral sex until he behaves. And if he doesn't, withhold all sex, buy a new vibrator, and use it in front of him. If that doesn't work, change the locks and get a life!

Note to Self: Don't play hard to get—play hard to keep!

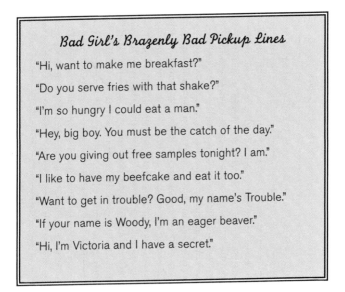

Bad Girl's Brazenly Bad Pickup Lines

"Hi, want to make me breakfast?"

"Do you serve fries with that shake?"

"I'm so hungry I could eat a man."

"Hey, big boy. You must be the catch of the day."

"Are you giving out free samples tonight? I am."

"I like to have my beefcake and eat it too."

"Want to get in trouble? Good, my name's Trouble."

"If your name is Woody, I'm an eager beaver."

"Hi, I'm Victoria and I have a secret."

find my passion and pursue it. I want a heated romance with a beautiful black

where to meet babes
on the fly

No bad girl worth her pantyliners needs a man. But hey, let's face it, there are times when you want one—and you want him fast: when you're opening a jar, moving heavy furniture, hunting for the source of that mysterious rattle under your hood, or fishing for your G-spot. Be prepared to survey any scene and spot your opportunity—you never know when your next man hankering will kick in.

Traffic Jams

Traffic is the most underutilized pickup scene in America. Think about it! You're alone, you're bored, you only need one hand on the wheel, and you've got a captive audience. Traffic is the ultimate meet market. It's window-shopping at its best. It's a babe browse-o-rama. The next time you're stuck in traffic, make eye contact and make the most of it. Your kids will love hearing the story of how you met.

The Overt Flirt

Establish eye contact with a cutie in a nearby car. Smile and wink or seductively lick your lips. Then wave something, whatever's close—your hand, your black lace undies, your tongue. If you get the desired response, flash your Ping-Pong paddle sign, "U SINGLE?" If he nods, flip your sign and flash him your phone number.

man. I want to be an architect. I want to live for years in Italy and study art. I

With a little planning and a good arm, you're golden. Write your number or email address on a sexy little thong or pair of panties and keep them in your car. (Finally, something to do with that damn thong you only wore once!) If you spot a babe with his window down or sunroof open, just lock and load. When your number sails into his life on silk, satin, or microfiber, he will call.

The Covert Flirt

If the overt flirt isn't your style, don't fret—let somebody else do the work for you! Keep a Sharpie in your glove box at all times. In a pinch, you can scribble your measurements and number on a banana (or other suggestive object). Smile at the toll taker and ask him to give this special item to the foxy man in the car behind you.

Other Great Places to Meet Men

Traffic school

Traffic court

While performing hours of community service picking up trash along the highway

The local auto body shop

want liposuction. I want to be a rock star or date a rock star. I want to have

American Men

If you want to snag a red-blooded American guy you've got to think like one. Fortunately, it's a simple recipe: Sex, Cars, and Sports. Naturally, there are many variations on these themes—and combo platters that men love, such as car sports, sports cars, sex in sports cars, sex in any car, sporty cars that get you sex, sport sex, sex while watching sports on a big-screen TV, and of course, sports that allow straight men to hug, grab ass, and jump all over one another without actually having sex.

Note to Self: Visit car wash. Good place to check out what he drives—and what he does when he thinks no one is watching.

How to Have a Foreign Affair

It's helpful to have a few handy phrases memorized to break the ice when traveling in a foreign country or encountering foreigners at home.

When in France . . .

Excuse me, do you speak bad girl?
Pardonnez-moi, parlez-vous mauvaise jeune fille?

Is that a French fry in your pocket or are you happy to see me? *C'est une pomme frite dans votre poche ou êtes-vous heureux à me voir?*

Good evening, sir. Are you a virgin?
Bonsoir, monsieur. Êtes-vous puceau?

Does this wine go well with sex?
Est-ce que ce vin va bien avec la sexe?

really rockin' sex with Lenny Kravitz. I want to be Miss America. I want a house

Do you know how to clean French dressing from the sheets? *Savez-vous comment nettoyer la vinaigrette de la literie?*

When in Italy . . .

Excuse me, do you speak bad girl?
Mi scusi, parli cattiva ragazza?

Good evening, sir. Are you a virgin?
Buona sera, signore. È un vergine?

Would you please direct me to a man who is firm to the bite? *Vòglia, vi prego, mi dirigere verso un uomo chi sia duro al mordere?*

May I take you home?
Pòsso accompagnarti a casa?

Have I mentioned I am a gymnast?
Ho menzionato che faccio ginnastica?

When in Spain . . .

Excuse me, do you speak bad girl?
Discúlpeme, ¿habla usted mala chica?

Good evening, sir. Are you a virgin?
Buenas tardes, señor. ¿Es usted doncel?

Would you like to put your bull in my china shop?
¿Quiere usted meter tu toro en mi chinero?

Hello. I am having a sexual awakening. And you?
Hola. Estoy experimentando un despertamiento sexual. ¿Y usted?

in Tuscany. I want to grow veggies and have many lovers. I want to travel, buy

how to lose a loser

When out in the social swirl, most of us work so hard to be hip, attractive, feminine, and alluring that we never discover how much fun it is to be none of those things. Once you're in touch with your inner loser, you've got a fully loaded secret weapon that can get you out of any difficult social situation in a flash. If you're stuck in a pinch, try one of these personas—and their foolproof techniques—for guaranteed single status on any plane, train, or bar stool.

Note to Self: If he dances and dresses better than you, he's interested in something else altogether.

Kindergarten Kate

• Reach for your purse and ask, "Want to see a picture of my Beanie Baby collection?"

• When he says, "I'm Rick," say back to him, "I'm Rick." Repeat everything he says. Be sure to mimic his facial expressions.

• After your third drink, talk baby talk and punctuate every sentence by crossing your eyes.

• Stick peanuts/pretzels/olives up your nose, then eat them.

Earnest Ethel

• Take his hand, gaze into his eyes, and say, "I'm so glad we've met. I've been looking for a husband who could be a good role model for my hyperactive disabled son."

• While listening intently to his insanely boring story, start to drool. Continue to nod like you're really into every word he's saying until the spit strand hits the bar—then explain about your rare health condition—you drool when you get excited. Mention that you're thrilled to meet a man who doesn't mind.

• Sing "Where Have All the Cowboys Gone," then burst into tears.

• Make a huge stink when the flight attendant/bar waitress serves your meal: "I ordered the Wiccan meal. Of course I'm sure. I practice the craft."

Dirty Debbie

• Hum "You Light Up My Life" and slow-dance in your seat.

• Point your finger at him and say loudly, "Is that a stick of gum in your pocket or are you happy to see me?"

• Frantically scratch your scalp, then inspect your shoulders for moving creatures.

• Whisper seductively, "Let's go back to my place. I'm so horny. I haven't seen any action since I had my genital warts burned off."

• As you walk away from him heading for the bathroom, launch into a deep-dig butt scratch. (Go for the gusto—and anything else that might be caught between your cheeks.)

want a sense of purpose and accomplishment. I want to be a torch singer in a

Bad Girl in a Bag
The 60-Second Undercover Disguise

Your date is boring you to tears, or some skankster won't stop buying you beers, or you just noticed your beautiful ex-boyfriend dancing with a boy who's way prettier than you. Suddenly you want to get lost in the crowd. No need to panic—you've got Bad Girl in a Bag!

Casually grab your purse and slip off to the ladies' room or a nearby pay phone. When you return—undercover—you'll be free to go or free to stay and go unnoticed.

What you need:

* a pantyliner
* a Sharpie
* scissors or a Swiss Army knife
* 60 seconds

What you do:

a) Color the entire panty liner with the Sharpie—black is more plausible, but if you're Irish, green makes a statement!

b) Cut out big eyebrows, a mustache, and a beard. (See diagram below.)

c) Peel off adhesive backing and stick to face.

d) Get lost in the crowd and go for it.

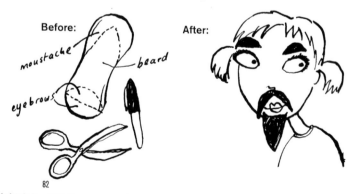

Before: moustache beard eyebrows

After:

nightclub. I want my mom. I want a white rabbit-fur jacket and to be a good girl

Things to Do with . . . Pantyliners

* Stick to handle of your luggage for easy identification at baggage claim.

* Add cushioning to any phone receiver for hours of pain-free shoulder cradling.

* Soak in perfume, essential oils, or flavored Kool-Aid and stick to the side of your toilet or hang from the rearview mirror in your car.

* Spray with glass cleaner, stick to your hand, and clean computer monitor.

* Absorbent, deodorizing shoe lifts.

* Stick to car antenna to find your car in a flash in the parking lot at the mall, stadium, or airport.

* Computer mouse cozy.

* Write "BROKEN" with juicy red pen and slap across a parking meter.

* Stick to back of hand to discreetly mop brow during stressful presentations or speeches.

* Disposable gym slippers.

* Use as a name tag at social mixers to stand out in any crowd.

* Barbie shawl.

and to run faster and do more push-ups than boys. I want to still be in love with

Stylin' Self-Defense Tips

Sneak Attack Action

When you're out on the prowl, you have to keep your wits about you, trust your gut feeling, and always be prepared to make a run for it. The element of surprise can give you the time you need to make a safe break from a bad scene. With a little planning you can assemble a small arsenal of sneak-attack weapons that look innocent but pack a punch.

Whoopee Cushion

Keep a loaded whoopee cushion handy when walking through a deserted parking garage or alley. If anyone scary approaches, just aim, squeeze, and run for it.

Sweaty Gym Clothes

If you happen to have your gym bag with you, keep your soggy, smelly sports bra or spinning shorts wadded up in one hand. Jam them in the face of any potential creep. If the stench doesn't stop him, yell, "And I've got crabs!"

Burp and Blow

If a pushy pedestrian tries to invade your personal space, conjure up a stinky burp and discreetly blow it in his face.

my husband.   I want a trampoline.   I want natural beauty.   I want to love and be

for Girls on the Go

Party Popper
Aim it in his face, pull the string, and suddenly the party's over!

Cheap Perfume
A shot up the nose or in the eye is a direct hit every time. (Great way to use up that cosmetic counter gift-with-purchase crap.)

Roshambo! Gotta Go!
Think rock, scissors, paper—and run for it!

Rock (fist to the ear or groin, hard!)
Scissors (fingers poked in the eyes, hard!)
Paper (karate chop to the throat, hard!)

Wad of Wasabe
The next time you eat sushi, take a wad of wasabe with you in one of those little plastic containers and keep it in your purse. If anyone gets too close, just jam wasabe up his nose, in his eye, or down his throat. And yell, "Burn, baby, burn! Sashimi on you!"

Karate Kicking Mule
If you're wearing mules, plant yourself firmly, keep your center of gravity low, and fire off a high-velocity karate kick at his head. Then watch your mule kick him between the eyes.

loved by someone, like there's no tomorrow. I want to be Harriet the Spy. I want

how to increase
your market value

The most powerful secret weapon you have is a man's imagination. Use it wisely.

The Double Date

Set up two dates with two different guys at the same time on the same night. Think of it as comparison shopping. You get to see who shows up on time, who's dressed to impress, who can handle himself gracefully under pressure. Of course, you act very apologetic, double check your date book, and then just see what happens. If there's a chance one guy may not show, set up a triple date. Just in case. Be sure to mention Darwin—remind them it's survival of the fittest.

Just Friends

Make sure you have a strikingly handsome male friend in your life to parade around in places where your target is likely to be around. Just buy him dinner and a few drinks and offer to return the favor when he needs a babe on his arm to make someone else jealous. If anyone asks, say with a smirk, "Oh, we're just friends."

Note to Self: Learn how to fall in love without giving up yourself—or your apartment.

to take Kelly, from Charlie's Angels, and Laura Ingalls Wilder out for a wild night

Booty-Call Waiting

If you're talking on the phone to a guy you want to want you bad and another call beeps in (or maybe you just pretend there's a beep), very casually say, "Can you hang on? I've got booty-call waiting." Then take the call (or put him on hold) for a good 30 to 60 seconds so he has plenty of time to ponder you and your in-demand booty. When you go back to him, say, "I'd really love to finish this conversation, but I have to get ready." His imagination will do the work for you—and he'll be wanting you bad all night long.

Special Delivery

If you're trying catch the attention of a guy at work, send a big, beautiful bouquet of flowers to yourself at the office and include a mysterious, romantic note from your secret admirer. (Okay, so it won't be a secret to you, but it will be to everyone else.) Leave the note in plain view on your desk.

Note to Self: Love means never having to say you'll swallow.

on the town. I want to work at a fashion magazine in New York City. I want a

Men and Directions

A man will never ask for directions if he's lost—much less admit it. That's why every bad girl needs to know how to satisfy herself and give clear instructions! If you fake an orgasm with the same guy more than once, you have no one to blame but yourself. Most men simply don't know when they're really satisfying a woman. It's not that they don't care, it's just that they have other things on their mind—their own satisfaction—and they simply don't know the terrain. If he seems lost, then he is. Try to talk him down like an air traffic controller helping a flight attendant land a plane. If he is too klutzy to deliver the goods, then take the wheel and drive yourself home. Automatic or manual transmission will do the trick—your dexterity will astound him either way.

Men and Diminished Expectations

Don't let erectile dysfunction ruin the mood! If your man is having trouble holding up his end of the deal, be a good sport and ease his tension. Guys love a playful whispered joke, especially when the chips are down.

* Looks like this dog won't hunt.
* I can't make a mountain out of a molehill.
* Looks like you're one slice short of a loaf.
* Onward and upward!
* Sometimes waiting is the hardest part.
* Are you down for the count?
* This is more fun than watching grass grow.
* At least I make your hair stand on end.
* The bigger they come, the harder they fall.
* Should I let sleeping dogs lie?

Barbie Camper Wagon.   I want a tattoo.   I want a boy to like me and never be

Better Than Bed

Once you get the date, why not make a first impression that'll last a lifetime?

Trampoline	The motion of the ocean without the sand in your crack!
Motorcycle	He rides the cycle, you ride him. It's the ultimate joyride!
Vineyard	Fun Adam-and-Eve costume opportunities!
Hot Tub	Love those jets. Millions of rubbing bubbles!
Carnival Rides	Centrifugal force! Oh yeah.
Elevator	Going down? Just keep one foot on the Close Door button.
Rooftop	When you're craving a little open-air shaft!
Laundromat	Washing machines vibrate more than a Magic Fingers bed!

Diamonds Are a

Is he marriage material or mirage material? Put any man under the microscope and find out the answer! The tried-and-true Four C method—clarity, color, cut, carat—will help you calculate the value of your potential mate before you take the emotional plunge.

Clarity *(the clearness and purity of the man)*

	Flawless	Partly Cloudy	All Smoke & Mirrors
Clear communicator?	❏	❏	❏
Clear thinker?	❏	❏	❏
Clear condom user?	❏	❏	❏
Clear intentions?	❏	❏	❏
Emotional clarity?	❏	❏	❏
Clear about my needs?	❏	❏	❏

Color *(the range and intensity of color in the man)*

	My Absolute Fave	Tired & Trendy	Would Need to Be High to Enjoy
Color of teeth?	❏	❏	❏
Car color?	❏	❏	❏
Color of his dress socks?	❏	❏	❏
Color of his sheets?	❏	❏	❏
Off-color sense of humor?	❏	❏	❏
Favorite pro team colors?	❏	❏	❏

Man's Best Friend

Cut *(the proportions, symmetry, and polish of the man, which determine his fire and brilliance)*

	Perfect	Sharp Enough	Dull as a Butter Knife
Dazzling wit?	❏	❏	❏
Cut bod? (above the waist)	❏	❏	❏
Cut bod? (below the waist)	❏	❏	❏
Dazzling eyes?	❏	❏	❏
Cut of his suit?	❏	❏	❏
Can he cut a rug?	❏	❏	❏
Haircut?	❏	❏	❏

Carat *(the unit weight of the man)*

	Mack Daddy	Average Joe	Lightweight
Can discuss weighty topics?	❏	❏	❏
Weight of his unit?	❏	❏	❏
Weight of his job title?	❏	❏	❏
Weight of his wallet (including photos of you)?	❏	❏	❏
Weight of his portfolio (pre IPO)	❏	❏	❏
Weight of his portfolio (post IPO)	❏	❏	❏
Weight compared to yours?	❏	❏	❏

The Four C Method Results:

Most of your answers in **first col**: Can't live without him!

Most of your answers in **second col**: Can learn to love him.

Most of your answers in **third col**: Can't believe I just wasted this much time thinking about him!

After the Date: Are You Really in Love?

Is it destiny, desire, or desperation? Is it love, lust, or location, location, location? How do you know for sure if what you're feeling is the real deal? Easy. These simple checklists will help you decide if it's a fabulous romance or a fatal attraction.

Checklist A

☐ You read the sports page before the entertainment section.

☐ You develop a keen fascination for plant spores, or whatever else he's into, to the point of taking a class—and boring yourself and your friends to tears.

☐ You offer to do his laundry for nothing in return.

☐ He asks you if you're outdoorsy and you buy an $800 mountain bike.

☐ Your bad girls get pissed because you're not returning their phone calls.

☐ You volunteer to cook dinner for a bunch of guys and watch *Monday Night Football,* your new favorite show.

☐ You use the words *soul mates* seriously in a sentence.

☐ You don't shove him out of bed when he snores like a snorting hog.

☐ You get kind of excited when his dog humps your leg.

If you checked 6 or more, this isn't dating, this is hell. Go back to chapter one and get into the Bad Girl Swirl. If you checked 5 or fewer, go to Checklist B—you might still find true love!

teased at school by anyone. I want a loving, kind, affectionate man that worships

Checklist B

- [ ] You lose 10 pounds while eating five steak dinners a week.
- [ ] You make your beloved pet sleep on the floor—for the first night.
- [ ] You start buying beer.
- [ ] You don't mind what you see when you look in his ear.
- [ ] You let him shave your legs.
- [ ] You add his number to your speed dial on all three of your phones.
- [ ] You forget to pay your bills—even though you have the money.
- [ ] You think men who burp and fart are suddenly kind of cute.
- [ ] You actually want to meet his mother.
- [ ] You agree to attend a wrestling match—as a one-time-deal only.
- [ ] Your orgasms are effortless.

If you checked more than 6, you're on the right track—but make him work harder for your love! If you checked 5 or fewer, keep trying—you may need a bigger dating pool. If all of the above apply, you're a big winner! It's the jackpot—true love. Congratulations.

the ground I walk on. I want boobs. I want to skydive. I want to look flawless

Getting a Job

3

A job is basically school for grown-ups. You dread it, you complain about it, you try to avoid going. But the truth is, it's kind of fun—just like school. You get to sit at a desk and look busy. You get to pass notes. You get to gossip about people. You get to pick on people. You get to have secret crushes. You get to learn stuff if you pay attention. But the best part of having a job is knowing where you're supposed to be every day and what you're supposed to be doing, even if you aren't there doing it.

Job Satisfaction?

Job satisfaction is an urban myth—not because it doesn't happen, but because it's not enough. If you're a bad girl, you don't settle for mere satisfaction day after day. You set career goals that are meaningful to you—**job jubilation**, **job nirvana**, **job titillation**. Decide how you want to feel at the end of every day and don't give up until you find a job that does it for you. Aim high and outside, wet and wild, fast and easy, warm and fuzzy. Whatever feels good to you. Lock it in on your radar and go for it.

Note to Self: Nose job? Never! Blow job? Sometimes. Job bliss? Always!

in the nude on a Sunday morning.   I want unconditional love and loose hips.

Why You Really Want a Job

* You can't live with your parents forever.

* You get business cards.

* You get to dress up and buy more clothes.

* You'll go crazy if you never leave the house.

* You can meet lots of new people without having to date them.

* Someone else pays for your voice mail.

* You sound cooler at cocktail parties.

* You get to go out to lunch a lot.

* You have some-one else to blame for your stress.

* Paid vacations.

Extra Bonus: Free office supplies! For creative ways to use your boss's business cards, page 110; pilfered Post-its, see page 125; toilet paper, page 135.

career counseling

No matter what your guidance counselor told you, careers don't require planning. A career is something that will happen whether you want it to or not. A career is nothing more than a six-pack of jobs. Unless, of course, it's a twelve-pack of jobs. It's as simple as throwing all your work experiences together! So don't try to plan the whole thing—in fact, dealing with your career all at once can make you as sick as drinking a sixer. But if you take it one job at a time, the whole working thing goes down easy.

Worthy Career Goals
Say it loud and say it proud: "I want . . .

Job Joy	Job Jubilation	Job Ecstasy
Job Euphoria	Job Orgasm	Job Peace
Job Elation	Job Freedom	Job Thrills

Achieving job joy may not have anything to do with your job description—so don't sit around in your cubicle waiting for the satisfaction cart to wheel by. You have to make your own fun, create your own challenges, initiate your own office enjoyment. You've got to stir the corporate pot, think outside the box, and push the envelope. You are the CEO of your own life.

I want my own phone line.   I want phone sex.   I want to never wear pantyhose

Your Fab Job Finder

Your fab job will get your motor running and give you the chance to rise and shine. Not sure what type of job is fab for you? Just take an honest inventory of your best qualities. Then forget about them. Being a good girl will get you nowhere in the workplace. Instead, zoom in on your worst qualities, the ones that got you in trouble in junior high. No matter what your parents may have told you, your "problem" behavior is your greatest asset when searching for a job. You not only have tons of experience, you'll enjoy the real job satisfaction that comes from doing what you love—with the added perk of proving your parents wrong.

Your Big Prob	**Your Fab Job**
gossip constantly	public relations exec
boss everyone around	lawyer
sleep until noon	nightclub owner
criticize others	movie reviewer
eat too much	plus-size model
can't spell	graphic designer
always look for the negative	meter maid
won't get off the phone	publicist
drag your feet	postal worker
dress like a tramp	assistant fashion editor

Your Big Prob	Your Fab Job
act bitter, crabby, and depressed	middle management
talk nonstop about nothing	radio DJ
play with your food	chef
drive like a maniac	city bus driver
touch yourself in public	porn star
tell big lies	writer
get in people's business	gossip columnist
refuse to clean up	set designer
act out	star of nighttime soap
don't finish projects	freelance anything
take off clothes in public	stripper
make trouble in class	political activist
mumble	receptionist
refuse to follow directions	entrepreneur
total bitch	dominatrix

Paving over Your Résumé Gaps

If you're looking for a blue-collar job, you need real skills. But if you're looking for a white-collar job, all you need is a résumé. Essentially, a résumé is a creative writing sample, so the only real important part is to flex your imagination. With unemployment at an all-time low, it's never been easier to euphemize your job history. Employers don't really want to know what you've been doing—they just want to know if you're willing to humiliate yourself and how soon you can start. When filling in your résumé gaps, be creative and confident and you'll be résumé-ed in the shade.

What You Did Last Year	What You Say You Did
collected unemployment and watched MTV	media expert specializing in the youth market
spent six months in the state pen	six months on a meditation retreat
worked at Blockbuster	feature film distributor
answered phones	telecommunications consultant
sold cellular phones	air traffic controller
Gap sales associate	Gap model
stayed on couch in utter depression	studied interior design
got fired several times	business consultant
got stoned constantly	extensive pharmaceutical research

again. I want to be a nurse and to get kissed by the end of fourth grade. I want

What You Did Last Year	What You Say You Did
finished writing your lame novel	finished writing your lame.com business plan
got laid off (with severance package)	raised venture-capital funding for your Internet start-up
shopped yourself into debt	retail analyst
Lilith Fair groupie	guerrilla marketing expert for the young women's market
played computer games	redesigned Web sites
got divorced	dissolved a failing business partnership
backpacked around Southeast Asia	Pacific Rim new business development
watched every episode of *The X-Files*	worked in video-on-demand
lived at home with your parents	family therapist
worked at the MAC cosmetics counter	trend forecaster

a bigger salary and bigger boobs. I want my mother's legs and a great sex life.

Bad Girl Confessions

Bad Girl Confession #11

I had sex while dispensing advice to a client over the phone.

Bad Girl Confession #12

After my last review, I poured Diet Coke in my boss's hard drive.

Bad Girl Confession #13

One time I had a temp job in New York at a really snobby PR firm. They treated me like I was a nobody, so on the launch day of an exclusive new perfume, I stole the only bottle and gave it to a homeless lady in the Times Square subway station.

Bad Girl Confession #14

I did two competing CEOs in one afternoon. And I wasn't even looking for a job.

Bad Girl Confession #15

As an executive assistant to the CEO, I would listen to his voice-mail messages and write them down. When I heard one from his buddy about his new assistant (me!) who liked "to get it up the ass," I decided to forward the message to everyone in the entire company. Needless to say, I was soon offered the promotion that I had been wanting for a while. (I wasn't really going to sue him.)

Giving Good Interview

Only good girls are silly enough to sweat and suffer through a job interview. A bad girl knows a job interview is just a TV talk-show appearance in front of a very small studio audience. Think about it—they invited you! They want you to be there. You want to look good and sound articulate, you want sell yourself without trying too hard, and you want the audience to love you. Powder your nose, pretend you're a celebrity, and enjoy the Q & A.

Why? Because it's fun and it works.

If you feel like a star, you'll act like one. And when you act like you're on the A-List, people will think you are. It's that simple. You'll be negotiating a salary faster than you can say, "Well, Oprah, I'm glad you asked . . ."

TV Talk-Show Tips

* Use a little more makeup than usual but a lot less than Baby Jane.
* Wear solid colors instead of loud patterns or prints.
* Imagine wild applause when you enter the room, smile warmly, and nod with gracious confidence.
* Never look directly at the camera—video or security.
* Casually call the interviewer by his/her first name so everyone will think you're good buds.
* Keep your legs crossed to avoid flashing the audience.
* Have your talk points ready in advance.
* Think fast, talk faster, and keep your energy up.
* Flatter your interviewer. No matter how lame his/her jokes are, laugh anyway.
* Be excited and exciting (only the entertaining guests are invited back).

I want a man (duh!) who is my best friend (blah blah blah) and humongous praise

The Celebrity Spin Cycle

The really fun part of pretending you're a movie star, politician, or best-selling author being interviewed is the spin cycle. When you think like a celebrity, you get to put a positive spin on everything. If your interviewer asks you a question and you don't know (or like) the answer, forget about it—literally. Simply answer a different question without skipping a beat, just like the pros.

This is easier than it sounds. For best results, use the jump-start technique when spinning your responses. Pick up on a key word in the interviewer's question. Then repeat that word in the first sentence of your answer— while you answer a totally different question! Be sure to have your talk points ready. Then be confident, be enthusiastic, be shameless.

For example . . .

The question: How do you perform under pressure?

Your talk point: I am a team player.

Your answer: That's a great question, Dave. Pressure is the most exciting part of doing business. In fact, I live for pressure. Long to-do lists. Tight deadlines. Late nights. I love the smell of No-Doz in the morning! Pressure excites me, if you know what I mean. It's the great equalizer, it's the glue, it's what holds the team together. And it's exactly why I am a team player!

The question: Describe how you solved a challenging conflict in your previous job.

Your talk point: I am a responsible employee.

Your answer: I'm glad you asked that, Ricki. My previous job was a joyous experience filled with interesting chal-

lenges and conflict. During my tenure there, I learned that everyone is responsible for causing and solving their own conflicts, which is one of the many ways I distinguished myself as a responsible employee.

The question: Where do you see yourself in five years?

Your talk point: I am extremely detail-oriented.

Your answer: Terrific question, Montel. Five years from now, I'd love to be in your position, making the big decisions, overseeing every important detail about this company. Success is in the details, am I right? Oh yeah. How do I know this, you may be wondering? Because I am extremely detail-oriented.

Note to Self: If you don't get the job, there must have been a clerical error.

.... *At a job interview* ....

👍 Kiss retroactive ass by praising your boss and company like a shameless brown-noser

👎 Say *anything* negative about your current or previous employer

with a lot of cobalt blue tile. I want the latest KTEL hot-hits album and a new pair

getting ahead

The typical workplace can be a treacherous environment. If you really want to get ahead at the office, be aware of what everyone else wants—and give them the impression they might get it.

The Corporate Ladder Game

You want: to get ahead without losing your mind or your self-respect.

Your boss wants: you to do as much of his/her work as possible without giving you any credit or overtime pay.

Your boss's boss wants: to see everyone suffer for the bottom line—don't let this power player see you having fun.

The bitter, overweight, middle-aged middle manager wants: to punish you for being younger, more attractive, and more successful than she/he is—or ever was.

The client wants: you to hold his hand, suck his thumb, feed him, burp him, and put him to bed—for 30% less than your initial estimate.

Your assistant wants: your salary.

The receptionist wants: to firebomb the telephone.

The mail guy wants: some respect and some action.

of roller skates. I want a recruiter to call me up and offer me a dream job in an

How you work it is your business. But remember, you're not really winning the game if you compromise yourself in any way. These general guidelines are a good place to start when developing your workplace survival strategy:

1. Make friends with the people at your level or below you.

2. Make peace with the people above you.

3. Make out with anyone you want at any level, especially at the Christmas party.

Note to Self: Pretend to know—look it up in the dictionary later.

Note to Self: Life is not a race—unless, of course, you're way ahead!

At a job interview

👍 Make eye contact

👎 Make eye contact while licking your lips

exotic location. I want to be near retirement where I can travel, cavort, and find

Business Lingo 101

The quicker you pick up on the real meaning behind business buzzwords, the faster you'll get ahead.

The Buzzwords	The Buzz
I'd like to build on your point . . .	I totally disagree with you, but you're my boss.
Thank you in advance.	If you don't do this, I'm screwed.
We're launching another major initiative.	Your life will be a nightmare for the next six months.
I was out doing competitive research.	I was shopping.
We need to think outside the box.	We're desperate.
Thanks, I'll take that into consideration.	Your ideas are stupid and you don't matter.
We'll do some qualitative research and report the results immediately.	I'll ask my wife.
This is mission critical.	Your ass is on the line.
Due diligence!	I have an MBA!
CC me on everything.	I don't trust you for a second.
We have a change in strategy.	We have no idea what we're doing.

Goal Setting

Getting what you want at work begins with setting goals for yourself. Start with small goals that you know you can attain, in order to build your confidence. Then gradually increase your goals over time until you've got exactly what you want. If your goals evolve, you will too!

How Typical Goals Evolve

I want my own desk.
→ I want my own office.
→→ I want other people doing all the work so I don't have to sit in my office ever again.

I just want time to eat my lunch.
→ I want time to eat my lunch anywhere but at my desk.
→→ I want to eat long lunches in great restaurants with interesting, smart, funny, attractive people, on my expense account.

I want that guy's pen.
→ I want that guy's title and salary.
→→ I want that guy to fetch me coffee while I sit in my new office, which used to be his before I became a bad girl.

I want the bagel with sesame seeds at the Monday morning status meeting.
→ I want the chocolate-covered donut with sprinkles at the Monday morning status meeting.
→→ I want to send raunchy emails from my laptop at the Monday morning status meeting.

new trouble to get into.   I want a surprise proposal from a man and to be whisked

Things to Do with . . .
Your Boss's Business Card

* Pick your teeth.

* Write "Nice job, you idiot!" on the back and stick on windshields of badly parked cars.

* Fold up and jam under wobbly restaurant tables.

* Wrap up old chewing gum.

* Write "stop me before I kill again" on the back and mail to local newspaper. (Wear rubber gloves.)

* Use for kindling on camping trips.

* Blot lipstick.

* Tack to message board in bowling alley coffee shop in the "looking for love" section.

* Write "Hard-body hunk seeks same for fun and games. Let's play hide the salami!" on the back and litter in lobby of your office building.

If your boss is a woman and you really hate her...

* Go to bars and flirt with gross, dorky men. When they ask for your number, enthusiastically give them her card.

away to locations unknown for adventure–just like one of those Visa commercials.

Saying No without Saying No

Every job has its share of grunt work that you have to do or you won't get paid. But don't get suckered into doing anyone else's grunt work. No one gets a bad review for performing menial tasks poorly. So avoid them at all costs. If you think fast and bad, your boss won't even know you're saying no.

Your Boss Says	You Say
"Will you get me a cup of coffee?"	"I'd love to. At my previous job, I got coffee for my boss but I spilled it, scalding my tender, young flesh, and sued for 12 million dollars."
"Would you read this for me and highlight the good parts?"	"No problem. But I'm so hung-over I'm seeing two of you right now."
"Carry this portfolio to the gate, will you?"	"I'd be honored. But I may get hung up at airport security. I forgot to remove my ben wa balls again."
"Could you pick up my dry cleaning?"	"I could, but I don't think that's an efficient use of my time. Do you?"
"Would you reorganize the supply closet?"	"Okay, sure. But I should probably tell you I was locked in a closet for eight months as a child and small spaces give me violent flashbacks."

I want great friends, good times, laughter, and tight bonds with family members,

getting out of the office

Once you get a job, the next thing you'll want is a way to get out of going. Odds are, your employer doesn't offer sufficient vacation days to ensure your happiness and sanity. This is not an oversight, it's a test. Employers do this to see which employees are self-motivated and willing to take the initiative (top management material) and which employees are passive and willing to suffer month after month. The more mini-vacations you create for yourself (without reporting them to HR), the happier you'll be and the more you'll impress your boss as a real go-getter. Here are a few easy outs.

true love, healthy children, attention from God, and to experience the world under

"I'm on jury duty."

Be sure to make it sound really boring. Say something like, "It's a federal court case involving environmental protection statutes and sewage treatment. I'm not supposed to talk about it, but do you want to hear about it?" No one will know or care what the hell you're talking about. They'll run away down the hall instead of staying to ask you questions.

"I'm having minor surgery."

This works extremely well if you look really healthy. When the problem isn't obvious, people tend to imagine the most gross, disgusting things like hairy moles, hemorrhoids, and anal fissures—and won't even ask. If someone does ask, just shake your head and say, "You don't want to know."

"I'm at an off-site leadership seminar."

If they ask for details, say, "Oh, that's right. You weren't invited to participate. Sorry, I shouldn't have said anything."

"I have to go to traffic court."

If they ask for details, get instantly irate and start spouting obscenities about the cops, the establishment, and the no-U-turn conspiracy. Most people will quietly back away.

"I have an all-day client meeting in . . . Hoboken."

If you pick some hideous location, people will immediately feel sorry for you and be so relieved they don't have to go there that they won't even think to ask for details.

water by scuba. **I want to speak lots of languages and impress foreigners with my**

The Insta-excuse File

These bad insta-excuses are guaranteed to turn people off—and get you off the hook.

Bad Plumbing

"My toilet backed up, overflowed, and flooded my whole apartment."

Bad Shellfish

"I had oysters last night and one of them was very bad."

Bad Traffic

"There was a toxic chemical spill on the bridge. I'm sure you'll read about it in the paper."

Bad Timing

"I was just finishing my workout at the gym when this huge class let out and a pack of manic spinners invaded the locker room. I had to wait forever for a shower."

Bad Communication

"I was told the presentation was tomorrow at 3:00."

Bad Directions

"I was totally lost. Back in hunter/gatherer times, people always found their way back to the village—things sure have changed! I guess we can blame cars for that."

Bad Luck

"My car got towed for no reason."

Bad Karma

"Birdshit landed on me and I had to go back home to change."

Bad News

"My grandfather died (again). He was like a son to me."

slang and dirty talk. I want to go to Johnnies in St. Louis, Mo., and get the gigan-

The Buddy System

Make arrangements with a friend at work to be your baddy buddy. It's a win-win business relationship! If you're stuck in traffic or stuck under the covers, just call your office buddy and get her to turn on your desk lamp, turn on your computer, put a half-empty cup of coffee on your desk, drape your favorite sweater over the back of your chair, and do anything else to make it look like you've been working for hours. (Of course, you'll return the favor when she's running late.) When you finally do get to work, leave your coat and bag in your car or stash them with the receptionist, behind a potted palm, or with the newsstand guy in the lobby. (You can pick them up later when you go to lunch.) Then casually stroll in carrying only a pen and a file as if you've returned from a meeting. **Note to Self:** Check teeth after lunch.

At a job interview

👍 Claim you ate a poppy-seed bagel right before if they do a drug test

👎 Eat a poppy-seed bagel right before your interview

tic ice cream sundae called the Kitchen Sink. I want to forget about fat grams and

Office Enemies

Sure, some men can make your life miserable on the job. But sometimes men are the faux foe—your worst workplace enemy might be a sister! These nasty women have a career goal to make everyone else as miserable as they are. If you know how to spot them, you can learn how to work them.

The Ass Kisser

Identifying marks: Syrupy smile and brown nose.

Agenda: Make everyone else feel good and herself look good.

Hidden agenda: Make herself feel good and everyone else look bad.

Her game: Act like the perfect employee only in front of the boss.

Your game plan: I Spy. (Use a hidden recorder, tape or video, to capture the real her. Then anonymously play it back on your boss's voice mail or leave it cued up on the office VCR.)

get a Big Mac instead of a hamburger at McDonald's. I want to marry my college

The Buzz Killer

Identifying marks: Wagging finger and smug I-told-you-so grin.

Agenda: I want to protect you from getting in trouble.

Hidden agenda: I want to protect myself from seeing anyone have any fun doing things I don't have the guts to do.

Her game: Guilts you into playing by her rules.

Your game plan: Be a Bad Influence. (Cherry-pop her! She obviously hasn't yet experienced the thrilling rush of being a bad girl.)

The Back-stabber

Identifying marks: Lots of new friends but no true friends.

Agenda: I really want to be your buddy and help you get ahead.

Hidden agenda: I really want to be ahead and see your head on a platter.

Her game: To get your trust, then get your guy, your job, and anything else you value.

Your game plan: Ms. Information. (Beat her at her own game by feeding her fake info about what you really want.)

Note to Self: Pluck oddball dark hair growing out of chin.

Note to Self: Do not pluck or tweeze anything while driving.

At a job interview

Act like you want the job

Act like you need the job

---

boyfriend. I want to get into my choice of medical schools. I want to not get

The Alpha Mouth

Identifying marks: Loose lips and a wagging jaw. Always the dominant, most aggressive gossip in the group.

Agenda: Knowledge is power. Oh, and I really care about you and want to know what's going on in your life.

Hidden agenda: Gossip is my only power. Without it, no one really cares about me and I have nothing going on in my life.

Her game: Talk the talk and colonize other people's thoughts.

Your game plan: Feed the rumor mill until it jams.

The Nympho Man-hater

Identifying marks: Tight, short skirts and cleavage-loving clingy tops.

Agenda: Do every man in the office.

Hidden agenda: Undo every man in the office.

Her game: Lower the integrity bar for every other woman in the office.

Your game plan: Direct Male Campaign. (Sneak onto her computer and send an email that says, "Just wanted you to know I'll be getting my test results back from the clinic next week. I'm optimistic but I'll keep you posted." Be sure to CC all interoffice males.)

The Bitch

Identifying marks: A sharp tongue and two faces that are pretty enough to let her get away with being mean.

Agenda: I don't care who I step on on my way to the top.

Hidden agenda: I don't care who I step on on my way to the top.

carded when I go in a college bar. I want to look young enough to get carded

Her game: I'm not being critical, I'm helping you become a better person.

Your game plan: Dish it back as hard and as fast as it comes. (If you show her you're not intimidated, you'll let the air out of her bitch tire.)

The Manic Oppressive

Identifying marks: Sweaty brow, beady eyes, nervous tics. Often seen hyperventilating while running from cubicle to cubicle.

Agenda: I'm doing my job, which is very important.

Hidden agenda: If I add tons of drama to my job, maybe I'll feel very important.

Her game: Turn every project into a panic party, ride the adrenaline rush, and crash and burn in your office.

Your game plan: Laugh Therapy. (The more stressed and panicked she acts, the more you laugh at the absurdity of her behavior, until she gets it—and gets off your back.)

again. I want to move out of my parents' house after four years of living there in

working your image

In today's competitive business world, your professional success often depends more on how hard you work your image than how hard you actually work. And that's great news.

Image-building Ideas

Miss See-and-Be-Seen

Create opportunities to be seen with the big players in your office. If the powers that be are walking down a hall, start walking with them (even if you're not going their way). Say in a loud, clear voice, "Hi, you guys!" If they laugh, you laugh. If they stop, you stop. If they run, you run too. When people see you hanging with the big shots, they'll think you're a big shot too.

Miss Hard-to-Get

If you want people to think you're super busy and important, call yourself at work and leave a bunch of messages until your voice-mail box is full. When people call and hear the recording, "I'm sorry, this mailbox is full," they'll think you're extra special or important or both. Plus, people always want what they can't have.

Miss Big Cheese

When calling someone you want to impress, say, "Please

limbo. **I want to pay off my college and graduate school loans. I want to become**

hold for [your name here]." Then put the call on hold, hit speaker phone, and calmly say, "Hello." People will think you have your own personal assistant. And you do—it's you!

Miss Popularity
Page yourself often at the office, in convention halls, or at the airport when traveling with coworkers. When people hear your name over and over again on a loud-speaker, they'll think you're in demand and want you more!

Miss Overachiever
Make a sign that reads "Employee of the Month" and post it beneath a big smiling photo of yourself. Then hang it up in your office or cubicle. Proven to boost your morale and your office reputation, even if you work alone!

Miss Bed-head
If you want the interoffice males to think you're a wanted woman, dress like you're getting some action. Once or twice a week, wear exactly the same outfit you wore the day before and arrive at work a little later than usual. When you walk in the door, have a smile on your face and a glazed-donut look in your eye. If anyone asks about last night, just get smirkish and, of course, deny that anything unusual happened. For variety, wear the exact same outfit but replace your top with a man's dress shirt. If they think you're in demand, you are in demand.

Miss Insider-info
Whisper. Say a person's name, whisper some more, then throw in words like "layoffs," "liposuction," "knee pads," "butt stain," or "it's so sad."

Note to Self: Avoid wearing high fashion unless high.

a cool aunt to my five nieces and nephews.   I want the lyrics of "Muskrat Love"

Beautifying at the Office

Hard day at work? Last-minute date? No time to race home? No time for a manicure or a style cure of any kind? No problem. Take a quick spin through the office supply closet and you'll be looking hot and funky in a flash.

Eyes

Who needs eye shadow when you've got copy toner? Just a smudge of toner on your lids will add drama and intrigue to your authentic office self. Or go for something more festive like blue highlighter eye shadow. To finish the look, line your eyes (carefully) with a black or brown felt-tip pen.

Hair

Add streaks of style to your hair with blue, pink, orange, yellow, or green from your collection of highlighter pens. Or empty out the paper holes from the hole punch and sprinkle them over your hair, then spray with hair spray.

Nails

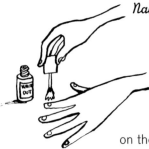

Dress up your nails with a quick coat of White-Out—then color them in with a cool highlighter pen. (Traditional yellow is better for meetings—go crazy with pink or neon green when you're headed out on the town!)

Note to Self: Never leave the house looking like crap unless you want to see him with his new girlfriend.

permanently deleted from my memory. I want to be president of my class. I want

Supply-side Accessories

Class up your after-work style with some sassy office
supplies.

* Rubber-band bracelets. (Wear them in bunches or
  add brads, binder clips, and paper clips for that
  charm-bracelet look.)

* Paper-clip choker with binder-clip drop. (The paper
  clips can hurt a bit. But hey, fashion is like that
  sometimes.)

* Matching binder-clip drop earrings.
  (Attach a binder clip to a paper clip,
  then loop through your hole. Mini clips
  for conservative girls or jumbo clips
  for fly girls.)

* Push-pin earrings in bright primary colors. (Just use
  pencil erasers as backs.)

* Binder-clip ponytail holder.

* Binder-clip cuff links.

* Style up that office frock with DSL line cord cinched
  at the waist.

* Add sparkle to your plain top
  with trim detailing of glitter and
  glue around the neck.

The Secret Power of Post-its

Post-its are not just a smart way to communicate with yourself, they're a super smart way to communicate with others, covertly. It's a fact: People read other people's sticky notes all the time. It's like sneaking a peek at someone's diary. It feels intimate and naughty, which, of course, is why everyone does it. Whether you want to plant the seeds for racy rumors or plump up your office image, go Post-it!

To enhance your office image, stick stealth notes to your desk, computer monitor, or butt with messages like . . .
  Meeting with George Lucas changed to Tues
  Levi's shoot postponed—tell Chad!
  Call in weed "prescription"
  Have e. ring sized
  Confirm flight to Rio

When submitting a report or written analysis, stick a few glowing Post-it notes to the document to influence the reader. For best results, disguise your handwriting.
  Brilliant!
  Insightful analysis!
  Hilarious! LOL funny.
  Kudos! This work deserves a bonus.

To get revenge without getting caught, go Post-it on someone else's computer. Messages like . . .
  Research STD symptoms online ASAP!
  Send Jan a Poo Poo special from Dogdoo.com
  Pick up Monica-style thong
  Renew NRA membership

to be a Rockette.   I want to be married.   I want to be in love.   I want to know how

Things to Do with . . . Post-its

* Boyfriend blinders—just slap one on each temple to prevent wandering eyes

* Emergency dandruff picker-upper

* Cover unsightly holes and stains on your clothes while appearing super organized

* Easy-to-pack disposable bikini

* Stick to nose to prevent a sunburn when sunscreen is out of reach

* Hold designer price tags safely out of sight all evening

* Color-coordinated place mats and napkin rings

* Stick to eyebrows for privacy when napping at work

* Different colored pads make festive cocktail-party coasters

* Mix and match mini Post-its into magnificent mosaic murals

* Cut into press-on nails when you need an instant manicure

If you have jumbo, presentation-size Post-its . . .

* Cheap window shades

* Stick one in front and one in back to make a sassy little strapless dress and heads will turn at the next office party

to tile my own bathroom.   I want a black leather jacket.   I want to believe in God.

Making an Impression at Meetings

Meetings are much more than an opportunity to interface and discuss projects with coworkers, they're forums for sexual fantasy. You won't read this in any employee handbook, but it's true! Meetings are unofficial social mixers where men and women of all levels get to come together and surreptitiously check each other out while pretending to do business. The hidden agenda in every meeting is mental multitasking. The big idea is this: articulate a coherent thought while mentally undressing the person sitting across the table and maintain your interested "I see your point" face as you imagine sucking earlobes and other body parts. If you're not working the sexual fantasy factor in a meeting, then you're missing the whole point of the meeting.

Meeting Management Strategies

The Fantasy File

Give your file folders provocative labels, such as "Favorite Positions," "Latest (Best) Offers," or "To Do (People/Places/Things)," and place them conspicuously on the table during meetings. Fantasy files add mystique to your office image and remind you—and everyone else—that you have a life outside of work.

The Bold Entrance

Avoid showing up at meetings on time. Arriving late to meetings proves to coworkers just how busy and important you are. When late, never slink in sheepishly or apologize like some wimp. Instead make a bold entrance that will enhance your bad-ass, power-broker image and

I want more, better sex. I want perfect skin and a blond ponytail and a shallow

inspire awe and wonder in the minds of everyone within earshot. Open the door a crack and finish an imaginary conversation, barking into your cell phone, then make a grand entrance. (If you don't own a cell phone, "borrow" one from an empty desk—just be sure to return it during a bathroom break before the meeting gets out.)

Say it loud and say it proud:

* "$50,000—and that's my final offer!" (Hang up.) "Moron."

* "Great, Ambassador. I'll meet you at the embassy at 7:30. Ciao."

* "I'm sorry, you'll have to discuss that with my agent. Please don't call this number again."

* "I don't care about the time difference. When I say sell, I mean sell!" (Roll eyes.) "Hong Kong."

If you don't have a cell phone handy, just act incredibly pissed when you make your entrance. For some strange reason, people imagine that really angry people are really important and must have really important things going on to make them that furious. Go figure. (No one will ever chew you out for being late if you're the angriest person in the room.)

Note to Self: Don't believe everything you read, especially when you write it.

The Silent Seduction

If you have no real power in a meeting, you'll want to exert your personal power over coworkers. Perfect the art of caressing a coffee cup, holding a pen provocatively, and nibbling on its end suggestively, especially if you have nothing relevant to say.

personality so I'd be perky and boys would like me. I want good coffee and the

boosting bad girl morale

Virtual Victory Lap

In the middle of an unchallenging, uninspiring work day, take a victory lap to lift your spirits. Run down the hall or around your cubicle, alone or with friends. As you approach the imaginary finish line, thrust out your chest to break the tape, then raise your arms high above your head and shout, "I win! I win!" When you sit back down at your tragically small and cluttered desk, listen for the thunderous roar of the crowd chanting your name. For best results, take a victory lap daily. You can mix it up by running around the block, running around the floor (be sure to push yourself when passing the boss's office), or running around and around your desk chair.

Primal Orgasm

Lead all of your female coworkers in a loud primal orgasm twice a day. Give points for realism, creativity, volume, and multiplicity. At the end of the month, the chick with the most points gets a standing O from her coworkers and a gift certificate for sexy lingerie or a sexy blind date. For best results, conduct a group primal orgasm when the big cheeses or clients are within earshot.

Note to Self: Chain letters and email are a complete waste of time, unless they affect luck, love life, or length of orgasm.

New York Times delivered. I want regular facials. I want to go to Europe and be

Chair Dancing

One working girl or many can enjoy the fine art of chair dancing. Improvise a stress-reducing solo or choreograph an uplifting routine for all the bad-for-business girls in your office and make Busby Berkeley proud.

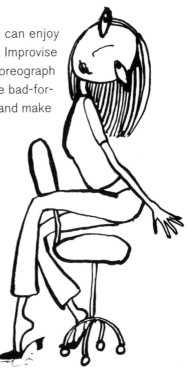

If your office chair has wheels . . .

* **Do the Push-back** (Think Esther Williams splashy!) As you roll backward, flutter-kick your feet and do a dreamy backstroke with your willowy arms.

* **Do the Spin and Kick** (Think Roller Derby meets the Rockettes!) Spin your chair and kick up your heels. Don't stop until you pull a muscle or run your pantyhose.

* **Do the *Flashdance* Flashback** (Think welder by day, dancer by night!) Get a running start, jump onto the rolling chair, and do your best steaming Jennifer Beals impression as you roll down the hallway.

If your office chair doesn't have wheels . . .

* Dance with your chair like it's the sexiest partner you've ever had and do a sweaty, sexy Flashdance for yourself and your coworkers. Extra points if it gets so hot that someone dumps a pitcher of water on you.

Anaïs Nin. I want relief from my crazy life of crime. I want smaller pores and

Copier Cotillion

Put a new spin on that classic office-party game of drunken photocopying. Play it during business hours when you're stone-cold sober! It gets the adrenaline pumping and the bad girl juices flowing. At the copier cotillion, you can come out in grand style, alone or with an escort. Keep your photocopies to yourself for a week or two, then have a bad girl power presentation to see who wins. The bad girl with the highest score gets to "Hide the Panties." (See below.)

Scoring:

  1 point for a cheek (face)
  3 points for a boob
  5 points for a cheek (butt)
10 points for two cheeks (one butt)
15 points for two cheeks (two butts)
20 points for two cheeks (face and butt)
25 points for a soft fleshy appendage
35 points for a hard fleshy appendage

Bonus Points:

  5 points for enlargements
10 points for color copies

Hide the Panties

One bad girl hides a pair of sexy black lace panties in the office of a senior employee. The others try to find them. To qualify as the winner, you have to not only find the panties but change into them—at the scene of the find. Proof of victory is your undies in the same hiding place where you found the black panties.

younger skin and sex. I want a Sting Ray. I want group sex in a shower. I want

Getting Off at the Office

* Buy a *Playgirl* or other stimulating magazine, hide it in a file folder, and read it in the middle of a meeting.

* Have phone sex with your honey.

* Wear tight jeans and rock back and forth in your desk chair.

* Put your pager on vibrate, slip it between your legs, and page yourself repeatedly.

* Instead of taking the elevator, take the stairs and slide down the banister—slowly.

* Press up against the copy machine while collating and stapling a big job.

* Go online and do a naughty key-word search.

* Pack a provocative photo of your lover in your lunch and moan with every bite.

Professional Poker

If you've asked for a raise and haven't gotten one even though you deserve it, then you need leverage. This may take some time and effort, but the payoff will be worth it.

Step One: Secretly look and apply for a job at a competing company. It doesn't even have to be a job you want; the point is to make yourself seem desirable—and worthy of a raise! At the competing company interview, inflate your current salary by 20 to 30 percent, and you'll feel extra good when they "top" your "current salary" to entice you away! Be sure to say you want to leave your old job because you want more responsibility and more challenges at work—not just more money.

Step Two: Get your new job offer in writing, then show it to your current boss. If your boss wants to keep you, he/she will have to match the new offered salary! Remember: You don't have to want to take the new job, you just have to act like you do.

If you play this well, you'll end up getting much more than the standard raise—and you'll get respect for your business savvy. If you don't get the raise, you can always get even.

a country house with a pool.   I want Terry Gross to want me.   I want a lifetime

Stuffing the Payroll Divide

Can't get the same salary as the men in your office who do your same job? Can't get the overtime pay you deserve? Can't get the raise you've earned? Don't get mad—get bad! It's time to even the score at the company store.

Most workplaces are stocked with essential supplies—paper, pencils, pens, paper clips, toilet paper, tissue, napkins, cleaning supplies, lightbulbs, salt, pepper, sugar cubes, Post-it notes, floppy disks, files, envelopes, staplers, scissors, glue, paste, brads, glitter. If you're not getting the compensation you deserve, devise your own payment plan. Don't stop with the little stuff. Be fair, of course, but be imaginative too. Think pencil sharpeners, potted plants, or that microwave in the kitchen. See a desk chair with wheels? Hello, dolly! Just load her up and you're good to go.

The Joy of a Bonus

One roll of toilet paper:	$ .59
One heist of toilet paper:	$ 11.21
One year of toilet paper heists:	$134.52

Knowing you'll never have to buy toilet paper again . . . priceless.

Pilfering Toilet Paper Like a Pro

Sure you can swipe one roll of toilet paper every day for the rest of your life. But where's the challenge in that? Where's the thrill? Where's the volume in the volume discount? Besides, it's kind of a buzz kill when you

supply of black tights.   I want a full scholarship for therapy.   I want a boyfriend.

reach into your bag after a few drinks at happy hour and a roll of TP flies out along with your business card and unrolls across the floor, stopping at the feet of the hot guy you were hoping to hook up with. It's far more fun to challenge yourself and stage a monthly TP heist when you're sure you'll be going straight home.

One roll under your hat.

One flattened in each bra cup.

One tucked into each armpit.

Six to eight threaded on a large belt around your waist under a coat.

One (wrapped in foil) on a long silver chain around your neck.

Two to four stuffed down your pantyhose if you're wearing a skirt or in your kneesocks if wearing pants.

Two to four (depending upon shoe size) taped to the soles of your shoes, transforming them into temporary platforms.

Note to Self: At next staff meeting, propose casual sex Fridays.

At a job interview

👍 Carry a briefcase or shoulder bag, even if it's empty

👎 Open your briefcase or shoulder bag, especially if it's empty

I want a girlfriend. I want government-subsidized tampons. I want perfect-fitting

Things to Do with . . . Toilet Paper

* Impromptu bandage when you need a quick sympathy vote

* TP a parking meter to save quarters

* Stuff bra (yes, this still works!)

* Super cheap mummy costume for Halloween

* Wraps nicely into a turban for exotic Middle Eastern look

* Tie between two chairs as a finish-line tape for victory lap

* Makes killer spit wads

* Desktop pillow for sleeping on the job (absorbs drool while you snooze)

* Play pass-the-roll at swinger parties

* Easy-to-grip spyglass (hold two and you've got binoculars!)

* Tape to steering wheel and dashboard (millions of tiny airbags)

* Sanitary in-flight headrest

* String a roll through your belt and sell by the square at concerts and ball games

black underwear. I want a cleaning lady. I want a partial lobotomy. I want self-

getting even

Bad Girl-illa Warfare

You don't have to behave badly to be a bad girl. Yet there are some bad situations when—after exhausting all the appropriate channels to correct the problem—all you can do is resort to Bad Girl-illa Warfare to get what you want and get the job done.

Bad Scene Asshole at work keeps sexually harassing you when you're alone with him.

Girl-illa Warfare When you're alone with him, grab him by the balls (hard!) and whisper "You've got to be kidding. I wouldn't waste my time with a Smurf dick like yours."

Bad Scene Client/Boss refuses to pay you money or overtime you are owed for services rendered.

Girl-illa Warfare Make a bunch of flyers explaining situation and stick them on the windshield of every car in the company's parking lot. Conclude with, "You could be next!"

Bad Scene Your incompetent, power-hungry boss continues to take credit for all your hard work and brilliant ideas.

Girl-illa Warfare Drop a sleeping pill in his/her coffee each morning. Gradually increase dosage until your boss

fulfilling bras. I want a new-love high that lasts more than nine months. I want gets caught sleeping on the job—and you get promoted.

Bad Scene You hate your job so much that you've alienated all hope of ever getting a good recommendation.

Girl-illa Warfare Simple! Duplicate your boss's signature on the scanner, then cut and paste it onto a letter you write yourself. Fax the letter to future employers and no one will ever know the difference!

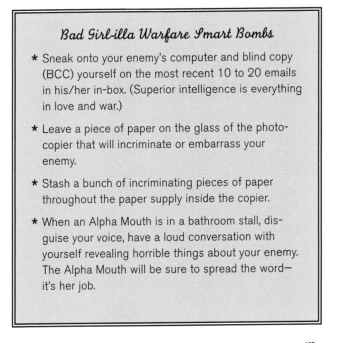

Bad Girl-illa Warfare Smart Bombs

* Sneak onto your enemy's computer and blind copy (BCC) yourself on the most recent 10 to 20 emails in his/her in-box. (Superior intelligence is everything in love and war.)

* Leave a piece of paper on the glass of the photocopier that will incriminate or embarrass your enemy.

* Stash a bunch of incriminating pieces of paper throughout the paper supply inside the copier.

* When an Alpha Mouth is in a bathroom stall, disguise your voice, have a loud conversation with yourself revealing horrible things about your enemy. The Alpha Mouth will be sure to spread the word—it's her job.

to be a ballerina or to know how to sing. I want to kiss a girl. I want glamour.

getting out

Reference Redux

If you need a current employment reference, give the name of a trusted friend or coworker. Make it clear that this is someone you work with on a regular basis but is not your boss. (In a confidential tone, tell your prospective employer, "Of course I don't want my current boss to know I'm job hunting. He/she would go mad with despair.") When your would-be employer calls your trusted buddy, the friend can vouch for your skills, professionalism, and work ethic—and even ballpark your phony salary. (Be sure to give your friend a cheat sheet with your "salary" and job description in advance.)

Interview Initiative

When looking for a job while you have a job, discretion is key. Keep a big shopping bag from a nearby department store or boutique folded under your desk. Tuck it under your jacket or inside a folded newspaper when you head out for an interview. Return to work carrying the shopping bag proudly (with your purse, your lunch, or a newspaper inside). If anyone notices your absence, just say, "Oh my God, great sale. You should check it out!" They may think you're irresponsible, but they'll never suspect you're interviewing.

I want to get out of New Jersey.   I want not to have to write any more English

Bold Bluffing

If people ask you if you're interviewing for other jobs, they may have noticed your strange, joyful behavior. Throw them off track immediately by telling them about your "new lease on life"—whether you blame it on a rejuvenating all-legume diet or your new witchcraft class, they'll back away slowly and stop asking questions.

Getting Free

Sometimes the only thing between you and real job joy is getting fired. Collecting unemployment for about six months gives you ample time to catch up on your sleep, see more of your friends, see more movies at bargain matinee prices, and figure out what you really want to do with your life. If you've been working for a couple of years, then you've been paying unemployment insurance, so you may as well take advantage of that and cash in.

The trick to collecting unemployment is getting fired. Fortunately, it's surprisingly easy to get the axe when you want it. Keep in mind that you may need to get another job at some point. So avoid committing any crimes or serious offenses that will prevent you from being hired in the future.

papers. I want to be recognized in my career. I want serenity. I want really sexy

Great Ways to Get the Axe
Performance Art
* Do an interpretive dance every time you wait for the elevator or copy machine
* Leave all voice-mail messages in rhyming couplets
* When you hear a phone ring, yodel in your cubicle
* Mime, anywhere, anytime
* Act out the instructions on the fax machine or fire extinguisher like an airline stewardess
* When asked a question in a meeting, answer by playing charades

Your calm explanation at your next job interview: "They didn't appreciate my job performance. Art is so subjective."

Be Weird
* Wear a down parka in the middle of summer
* Talk to and play with imaginary friends
* When asked to do something really demeaning, jump up and down and squeal, "Yippee! Yippee!"
* Don't wash your hair for a month
* Sit on your desk, cross your legs, and chant
* Speak only in pig Latin

Your calm explanation at your next job interview: "Creative differences."

gray hair. I want an Easy-Bake Oven. I want money, power, aphrodisiacs, a mois-

Talk Back

For example . . .

Your Boss: I think we have a problem here with your performance.

You: Nuh-uh.

Your Boss: You have become a bad influence.

You: Takes one to know one.

Your Boss: What's your deal? You're behaving like an unprofessional idiot.

You: I know you are. But what am I?

Your Boss: This has got to stop!

You: You started it! I'm not stopping until you stop!

Your calm explanation at your next job interview: "The corporate culture was extremely patriarchal."

Note to Self: If you're not scaring anyone, you're not being bad enough.

turizer that really works, and a body that stops traffic. I want my own apartment,

Getting a Life

Being a bad girl is not just a trendy lifestyle, it's a trendy way of living. But getting the life you want and having fun doing it is a trend that never goes out of style. Once you lock and load your bad girl self, you'll be getting what you want every day in every way—cool friends, the perfect pad, excitement, adventure, happiness, mental health, and emotional wealth. You'll get better parking, better perspective, and a better self-image. You'll get more free stuff, more free time, and more freedom to be all that you can be without ever joining anyone's army.

Why You Really Want a Life

* Little things don't bug you as much.
* You'll rule at your high school reunion.
* Justifies big bar tabs at swanky spots.
* You get to wonder who will play you in the movie.
* You talk to your parents less.
* Juicy journal entries make for great posthumous publishing.
* Perfect distraction from Why-Are-We-Here woes.
* You'll feel less guilty about your cell-phone bill.
* It won't take a month for someone to find you if you die in your sleep.

a horse, and to be 11. I want my own apartment, money, and to be 21. I want a

friends for life

When you're a bad girl, popularity is no contest. You are the in crowd, the It girl, and the star of your show. You've got your mojo, you're in the flow, your cheeks—both pairs—glow. When you're a bad girl, you're a babe magnet. Everyone wants to know you, be you, or do you—and feel that voodoo that only you do so well.

The key to a great bad girl life is great **bad-girl friends**. Choose them wisely. Your friends are your sounding board, your sanity savers, and your personal board of directors. They are your allies and your accomplices. They're your bad girl posse, your traveling squad, and your all-girl band. Your friends are the girls in your swirl. They will influence the way you walk and talk, how you think, what you drink, where you go, who you know, what you share, where you shop, and how you wear your hair. A real bad-girl friend is not only there for you—she's good for you.

Note to Self: Boyfriends go in and out of fashion, but friends never go out of style.

Bad Girlfriends vs. Bad-Girl Friends
Know the difference and how to deal.

A Bad Girlfriend	**A Bad-Girl Friend**
Thinks of you as a rival	Thinks of you as a rebel
Will steal your man if you're not careful	Will steal your drink if you're not careful
Talks about the size of your ass at work	Covers your ass at work
Will dump you in a flash if she gets a boyfriend	Will be there in a flash if you get dumped
Tells you it's immature that you want to do a drive-by	Rides shotgun when you want to do a drive-by
Tells you things she knows will hurt	Tells it like it is, even when it hurts
Flirts with your boyfriend	Farts with your boyfriend
Borrows your favorite outfits and returns them smelling smoky and stinky	Borrows your favorite outfits and wears them looking slinkier and sexier than you
Dates your ex without a second thought	Hates your ex without a second thought
Doesn't take any responsibility for her shit	Doesn't take any shit

A bad girlfriend is no friend at all. Lose her fast, and don't lose a minute wondering if you did the right thing. A bad-girl friend is a keeper. She keeps you laughing, keeps you strong, and keeps you in touch with your best bad girl self.

How to Lose a Bad Girlfriend

She slept with your ex (he started it!), borrowed and ruined your favorite sexy T, and never asks you how you are. If you've stopped returning her calls and inviting her to parties—but she still clings to you like wet TP to a leopard-print mule—it's time for action. One or more of these aggressive treatments should eradicate the problem in a flash.

Driving Miss Daisy Crazy

* Invite her to a movie, go for popcorn halfway through, and don't come back. When she asks you about it, say, "I was there. What happened to you?"

* Swipe her keys whenever you can, move her car, and return the keys.

* Call on her behalf and cancel her health club membership, phone service, or hot date.

Flirting with a Fashion Disaster

* Throw a swank cocktail party and tell her it's a '70s disco party. (If she confronts you, say "Didn't you get my email?")

* Throw a '70s disco party and tell her it's a formal black-tie affair.

* Throw a black-tie affair and tell her it's a hoedown.

huge tent to throw parties in. I want my own woodworking bench with a vise grip,

The Last Gasp Seduction

* Tell her the cute guy at the office/gym/apartment building is madly in love with her but too shy to say hello.

* Tell the office/gym/apartment building creepy loser that she is madly in love with him.

* Tell her whatever she's doing is working and you're madly in love with her.

National Lampoon's Permanent Vacation

* Offer to hang with her while she packs for her vacation and slip a metal pipe, a doobie, or other contraband into a pocket of her luggage.

* Take her with you on a road trip, dress up in bedsheets for a spontaneous toga party, and leave her beside the road in some redneck town.

* Invite her on a hardcore mountain bike ride after replacing her brake pads with baked teriyaki tofu.

Note to Self: Friends don't let friends shop drunk.

wood-burning kit, and assorted tools. I want a faster metabolism. I want a three-

Be a Bad Girl Mentor

Not every young girl is lucky enough to have a bad girl in her life. If you know a girl like this, a girl who may be at risk of becoming a good girl for the rest of her life, reach out to her and become a bad girl mentor. Just a few hours of your time each month can make a world of difference to a young girl in need of a positive role model. If you have the time and resources, take a few young girls under your wing and start a bad girl troop. You can encourage them to take on new challenges, learn new life skills, and not get suckered into playing by someone else's rules. When you become a bad girl role model in your family or your community, you discover that the best part of getting what you want is giving back.

Helpful Hints for Bad Girls in Training (BGITs)

Reward your young BGITs with a bad girl merit badge for every new skill or bad girl quality they master. This instills a sense of pride and accomplishment and makes learning as much fun as a game! Suggested BGIT badges:

* laughed at myself
* ran through the sprinklers in party clothes
* used loud fart whoopee cushion at a bar mitzvah
* bought expensive impractical shoes
* fooled someone with trick ring and squirted water up his/her nose
* danced around and found the boogie in my butt
* trusted my instincts
* blew up a Barbie

way in a four-star hotel.   I want to get my period more than anything.   I want to

The Bad Girl Party Planner

There's nothing better than spending quality time with friends doing the things you love. Choose one of these party themes for a fun-filled evening of bad girl bonding—or combine some or all for an unforgettably wild weekend!

Spa Night!

Trade off pampering each other with a bad girl beauty mask. It'll take years off your tired, stressed face and maybe even make you look like a teenager again!

What you need:

A big jar of mayonnaise

A large package of sliced bacon

Cheez Whiz

Hard sliced salami

What you do:

Wash face with cleanser and warm water, then pat dry.

Spread thin layer of moisturizing mayo all over face.

Cut a strip of raw bacon in half and slap across forehead.

Squirt Cheez Whiz on lips, covering all lip lines and chapped territory.

Place a salami slice over each eye.

Recline for 15 to 20 minutes.

After each beauty treatment, toss the mask ingredients into a skillet with chopped onions, peppers, and tomatoes and whip up a bad girl scramble!

Note to Self: Rehydrate early and often.

get out of college and work in publishing. I want my life to slow down a little so

Scavenger Hunt

Divide up into teams of three, head out on the town, and collect things like . . .

* a pair of men's underwear
* a stranger's bra
* a Polaroid of yourself and a con-senting adult in a compromising position
* a marriage proposal written on a cocktail napkin
* a Polaroid of a guy's butt with a lip-stick smooch print on it (the butt, not the Polaroid)

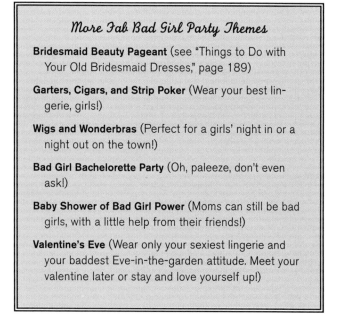

More Fab Bad Girl Party Themes

Bridesmaid Beauty Pageant (see "Things to Do with Your Old Bridesmaid Dresses," page 189)

Garters, Cigars, and Strip Poker (Wear your best lingerie, girls!)

Wigs and Wonderbras (Perfect for a girls' night in or a night out on the town!)

Bad Girl Bachelorette Party (Oh, paleeze, don't even ask!)

Baby Shower of Bad Girl Power (Moms can still be bad girls, with a little help from their friends!)

Valentine's Eve (Wear only your sexiest lingerie and your baddest Eve-in-the-garden attitude. Meet your valentine later or stay and love yourself up!)

I can catch my breath. I want to keep things interesting. I want to be arrested

Bad Girl Out-of-Focus Group

Answer these questions just like the bad girl pros who contributed to this book. It's really fun, always funny, and a great way to bond.

What you need:

This book

Free-flowing booze

What you do:

After a few drinks, read the following questions to all your bad-girl friends. When everyone has written down her answers, shuffle the cards and redistribute. Then go around the circle reading the answers out loud, one question at a time, and try to figure out who's who.

1. Who is your favorite bad girl?
2. What do you really want in life?
3. How do you get what you want?
4. What do you secretly want that you don't want anyone to know you want?
5. What did you (or will you) want most at age 10? 20? 30? 40? 50?
6. Complete the following sentence in as many ways as you want: *You know you really want it when . . .*
7. What's the baddest thing you've ever done to get what you want?
8. What's the baddest thing you've ever done . . .
   a. in a bar?
   b. in a car?
   c. in a cubicle?
   d. in your parents' bed?
   e. on a plane?

just once.   I want to be a famous artist.   I want everyone to loosen up.   I want to

How to Be a Bad Influence

Bad girl parties are the perfect occasions to exert your bad influence. Start by doing a little research to find out which of your friends are virtual virgins in certain activities.

Topics to explore:
* jaywalking
* calling in sick and going to the beach
* shameless shopping
* creative parking
* exhibitionism
* borrowing roommate's clothes
* kissing a stranger
* social stalking
* crank calls
* eavesdropping and retelling fab tales as your own

Once you know which friends are virtual virgins in which categories, you can begin a program of systematic cherry-popping until each girl has confronted her biggest bad girl fears and opened the floodgates to her badness. When your friends see how much fun you have jaywalking, parking on sidewalks, and stealing kisses from strangers, they won't be able to help themselves from joining in. Soon your friends will be returning the favor, teaching you new tricks, and challenging you to be badder than you've ever been before.

Unless, of course, they get in over their heads, get into big trouble, and suddenly need a ride home at 3:00 a.m., a good lawyer, an alibi, or all of the above, and never want to talk to you again. But that hardly ever happens.

go live in the country with lots of land with my cool hubby. I want an old GMC

Cheap Thrills

If you're constantly pulling pranks on others and yourself, you'll never experience a dull moment! Here are a
few ideas to get your adrenaline flowing.

* Display religious figurines in your cubicle, cross
  yourself before meetings, and generally pretend to
  be virginal. See how long you can keep your
  coworkers going.

* Do shots of espresso at parties instead of booze.
  You'll get the dance party started with the shakes!

* Wear S & M leather bondage gear to the dentist's
  office—or anywhere else you think the
  receptionist needs a pick-me-up.

* Light your farts on fire.

* Streak.

* See how many movies you can
  see at a multiplex theater before getting thrown out.

* Leave powdered Pop Rocks in a Baggie on the coffee table at a party and see if anyone goes for it.

* Crash wedding receptions at swanky hotels.

* Make yourself faint. (Stick you head between your
  legs, hyperventilate, then stand up really fast. Great
  for getting out of work, school, and blind dates!)

* Park in front of the main branch of the post office
  30 minutes before closing on April 15th and watch
  the madness. It's a real butt-pucker!

* Stay a few steps ahead of the meter maid and pump
  coins into expired meters right before she starts to
  write the ticket. It's a laugh and a half.

Immediate Gratification

The ultimate form of immediate gratification is simply deciding that what you have right now is exactly what you want. But that's too much work for most people. It's a lot easier perfecting the art of denial. Some people can live permanently in a state of denial—the 51st state of America—and many settle down there without knowing it. As a bad girl, your job is to know exactly where the state of denial is on the map and take short visits when you need to—without staying for good!

Denial—the 51st State of America

Come for picturesque views, stay for all the friendly people.

To develop your personal denial skills, study your parents or any seemingly blissful adults who are clearly out of touch with the boring or hard realities of their lives. Model yourself after the ones you respect most. You can accelerate quickly up the steepest learning curve by practicing denial-inducing phrases like these:

"Fine thanks, how are you?"

"It's not an addiction, it's a prescription."

"Pants are sized much smaller these days."

"I am listening to you. I'm just looking at the TV."

"Affair? What affair?"

"Why would I go to therapy?"

"Bored to death? Nah, I'm just always tired."

"I only use my credit cards for emergencies."

"Sex doesn't interest me anymore."

"Pass the Chardonnay."

Note to Self: Never return a Publisher's Clearinghouse Sweepstakes form no matter how bored you are.

pickup with flames painted on it. I want to be the queen lounging on a red velvet

Perception Is Everything

If you can't find the state of denial—or get what you want pronto—simply adjust your perception of who you are and what you have. With a quickie mental upgrade of your reality, you can feel better about your life in seconds.

Your Reality	Your Mental Upgrade
I live in a basement.	I live in a garden apartment.
I can't balance my checkbook.	I'm a creative genius.
I work out of my studio apartment.	I work in suite 7B.
I'm flabby.	I'm fluffy.
I'm broke.	I have a cash-flow problem.
I'm between jobs.	I'm on hiatus.
I'm a pathetic loser.	I'm an artistic loner.
I'm a temp.	I'm a mercenary in the war against data processing.
I'm always single.	I'm too independent to be in a relationship.
I can't afford to do laundry.	I'm so boho chic.
I have no idea what I'm doing with my life.	I'm a free spirit.
I'm wearing clothes with holes in them.	I'm so retro!
I lost again.	Contests are stupid.

bed while sexy slave boys feed me peeled grapes. I want to be strong and a good

Action-packed Commentaries for Those Inevitable Boring Moments

Commentate your way through dull everyday events to feel like a star in no time!

* "The tension is high here at the Saturday Night Solo Couch-surfing Invitational!"

* "Anything can happen, it's Extreme Freestyle High-attitude Mopping!"

* "Thanks for tuning in to the International High-drive Carpooling Competition!"

* "Stay tuned for Mach-speed Masturbating Madness!"

* "Yes, it's the Packing for 10 Pre-vacation Countdown!"

* "Up next, big-time Power Procrastinating! You won't believe your eyes!"

* "Yes, it's the end-of-the-month Fridge-o-rama Fight for the gold through the old and the mold!"

* "Welcome to the Buying More Lottery Tickets like a Loser Fool Final Four!"

* "Don't blink or you'll miss our Sky-cam Eating over the Sink Special!"

* "Welcome to our live coverage of the Big Mack Daddy Morning Commute!"

* "Sit back and relax! It's time for the Cereal for Dinner Again Super Bowl!"

A Winning Attitude

How you feel about your life depends as much on your attitude as your reality. And that's great news. You can change your attitude faster than anything else—and it's free!

Attitude Adjusters

Dance Therapy

Some mornings—no matter how bad you've been—it just happens. You wake up on the wrong side of the brain and feel like caca. You can go back to bed or suffer your own evil mood all day—or do a self-intervention and dance yourself happy! Forget about your morning routine, crank some favorite dance tunes and slowly begin to wiggle. Then dance around the room until you feel your butt start to giggle. Keep dancing for as long as it takes until you've got a big smile on your face and the boogie in your butt. It's your bad-girl power point and it'll keep you charged throughout the day. And honey, shake it, don't break it.

Stop Thinking!

Recent studies reported in real live medical journals indicate that there is no such thing as a stressful life event—only stressful thoughts about life events. Therefore, if something upsets you or makes you nervous, stressed, or freaked out in any way, just don't think about it. The way to eliminate stress from your life is simply to stop thinking. Hurray! One less thing to do.

Take 10 Years off Your Age

The only way to stay young forever is to lie about your age early and often. Lying about your age is a lot like using eye cream—by the time you realize you need to do

ice-skater and a good artist. I want unconditional acceptance and support from

it, it's way too late. Start when you're very young, like in middle school, and keep people guessing for the rest of your life. The best time to change your age is right before a life transition—a new school, a new job, a new relationship, a new city, a new face—don't be afraid to subtract a whole golden decade. If anyone calls you on it, just say, "Must have been a typo!"

Note to Self: You're not just getting older, you're getting bitter. Lighten up!

Note to Self: Make friends with people older and more wrinkled than you.

Smile Therapy

If you're feeling super crappy, crabby, or cranky, smile like crazy at everyone. Small children, small animals, and adults of all sizes will smile back at you, which may make you feel better. But what's even cooler is this: if you smile a lot when you're totally stressed or depressed, you'll feel like a raving lunatic, which is kind of demented but really fun for variety and will definitely make you feel better.

Dress Yourself Happy!

Feeling down? Don't lounge around in smelly sweats and the T-shirt you slept in, dress up! Put your hair up, put your face on, then slip into something sexy, chic, or sophisticated and get out of your head and out there in the world. A personal power outfit should be constructed like a skyscraper—from the ground up. So start with a solid foundation—and the right pair of shoes—and build up from there.

Note to Self: If I love it and it fits perfectly, don't think about it. Just buy it.

my mom. I want a drum set. I want to be an anonymous celebrity. I want to be a

bad is beautiful

Mirror, mirror on the wall . . . bite me!

When you're a bad girl, you are beautiful, every day in every way. Bad hair? Love it! Stressed out? Intense! Bad skin? Fabulous, darling! Dark circles? Dramatic! Show yourself some love. Start with a modest daily affirmation to awaken your self-esteem.

The 13 Sacred Bad Girl Affirmations

When you look at yourself in the mirror, lovingly say to your reflection . . .

1. "Good golly, I'm a hot tamale!"
2. "I declare, I dig my hair!"
3. "It's hip and funky looking this damn chunky!"
4. "It's no paradox that I am such a fox!"
5. "Tell your Mom, I'm the bomb!"
6. "Don't mean to be crass but I love this ass!"
7. "Hot home cookin'—I'm that good lookin'!"
8. "With eyes like mine, who needs wine!"
9. "I heart my pores like warm s'mores!"
10. "Strike a pose, 'cause I adore this nose!"
11. "It's super heavy duty, being such a freakin' beauty!"
12. "You're so purty, let's get flirty!"
13. "Oh yeah honey, I'm so money!"

radical filmmaker and I want everyone to know my name, but I don't want anyone

Nice Booty, Baby!

The next time you get a compliment, keep it! Take it to heart—and take it to the bank, where it can accrue for you. This goes for compliments at work or on the street, whether from friends and lovers or strangers and cat-calling construction workers. It's easy and fun to create your own **compliment bank**. Just fill a small card file with index cards and make tabs for your most popular features, such as:

My Brain
My Butt
My Sense of Humor
My Hair
My Style
My Legs
My Walk
My Everything Else

Whenever you get a new compliment, write it on an index card and deposit it in your compliment bank. Keep your compliment bank handy on your desk or on the back of the toilet. When you're feeling low or doubting yourself, just check your balance. A quick review of your compliments and you'll feel loaded with self-love and maybe even a splash of self-lust.

Note to Self: Tell the biggest pores you love them.

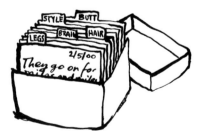

to bother me in the grocery store. I want Madonna to want me, then I'll turn her

Getting Some TLC

Feeling starved for affection? Missing the human touch? Sure, you can just get drunk and sleep with your ex or some other convenient guy. But why not practice public displays of affection with strangers instead? Anonymous PDAs are quick, safe, and far less complicated than any other way of secretly getting another human being to touch you and show you some love.

Perfecting the PDA

* Fake a knee injury at the gym so a hottie trainer or sports doctor will feel up your leg.
* Ride crowded subways, trains, and buses at rush hour for that group-hug effect.
* Go into Victoria's Secret and ask to be measured for a new bra.
* Bump into people on purpose, then grope them lovingly as you apologize.
* Step into jam-packed elevators every chance you get and ride up and down until the crowd thins.
* Go to sample sales and stand still next to anything cashmere.
* Instead of shaking hands with business colleagues, greet them with a kiss and a warm full-body hug.
* Take a yoga class and do all the poses wrong so the instructor will gently correct you.
* Go to a service at any temple, church, or place of worship where you get to hug all the people around you.
* Get pulled over, then act belligerent and paranoid until you get patted down and cuffed.

down because I'm in love with my girlfriend. I want to be Sinead O'Connor, but I

Quick Pick-me-ups

I want to feel appreciated

Pop into a bookstore and casually browse the hip, popular books near the counter. Suddenly, let out a high-pitched squeal of joy and say in a clear and loud voice, "Oh my God! You carry my book!" If no one responds (or gives a damn), say it again, louder. Accept any praise directed your way and take it to heart, then graciously offer to sign copies of the book. For best results, choose a book without an author photo. (Pssssst. This book has no author photo. Go for it!)

I want to feel popular

When walking past a big group of attractive people who seem to be having tons of fun (in a bar, on the street, at a picnic), wave and yell, "Bye, you guys!"

I want intelligent, stimulating conversation

Talk to yourself.

I want to feel pampered

Practice platonic dating. Go out with other girlfriends who are single and pamper yourselves—instead of just trying to meet guys. Catch a chick flick, enjoy a quiet dinner at a deluxe restaurant, order a fabulous bottle of wine, go to a swank gallery opening, get away for a rustic bed-and-breakfast weekend, or park it poolside at a luxury hotel. You'll not only have fun, you'll be more appealing to others because you're having fun.

Note to Self: Practice kegel exercises at home before performing in public.

am afraid my head isn't well shaped enough to shave it. I want to make a killer

I want to get my picture in the local paper

    Get arrested for committing some ridiculous misdemeanor.

    Put dish-washing liquid in a fountain.

    TP a statue in the center of town.

    Climb way up a tree and refuse to get down.

I want to feel rich and powerful

Go shopping. Try on ridiculously expensive things that you could never afford. Glare back at the smug salesperson and say, "I'll take them." Charge up a storm—but only at stores that give a full refund with a receipt. Feel the power of the purchase, ride the retail rush to the edge of your credit limit. Then have a friend return all of your purchases the very next day. (Be sure you know your available credit so you don't charge over your card limit. A declined credit card will bring you down hard.)

I want to win every argument

Fight with yourself.

I want to get carded again

Go to a grocery store and buy cereal and booze, especially something fruity like Peach Schnapps. Works every time, no matter how old you are, and makes you feel like a million bucks!

narrative feature film that makes people think in a totally different way. I want to

landing the perfect pad

Depending upon your budget and where you live, getting the pad you want can be a breeze or it can be a depressing, humiliating, hopeless process that makes you doubt yourself, your credit history, your very reason for living where you do—and even make you want to move back in with your parents. Either way, a little bad girl brainstorming can't hurt.

The trick to landing the perfect pad in a competitive market is simply to stand out from the crowd. When looking for a new place, you have to dress for it. Figure how your competition will be dressed and play against type. Think of your bad girl icons. If your budget is downmarket, dress up—Holly Golightly swank or Oprah fabulous casual. If your budget is sky-high, dress down—Madonna skank (think *Desperately Seeking Susan*) or working girl Lucy Ricardo at the candy factory. If you look different from the maddening crowd, you'll be more memorable. And that's half the battle.

Beyond that, landing a fab pad pretty much boils down to bribery and kissing butt. When you meet your prospective landlord, the super, or whoever will be making the decision, you have to play Nancy Drew, girl detective. Look for clues that will reveal an Achilles' heel—which, of course, you will later try to pinch as hard as possible.

raise my family with my beautiful girlfriend on a beautiful organic farm some-

Is he wearing a Mets hat, a Sharks jacket, or a diamond pinky ring? Is she pleasantly plump? Is he popping the last bite of a cannoli into his mouth as he opens the door? Is she wearing a boatload of makeup? Note any hippie giveaways like tie-dyes or Birkenstocks. Perk up your ears—is that Sinatra, soothing ocean sounds, Smashing Pumpkins, or a video game console beeping? Use all your senses. Does he smoke cigars? If you can figure out what he/she loves, then you can pack up a personalized care package to deliver with your rental application.

Bribery Best Bets

* tickets to a ball game
* a homemade apple pie
* a plate of your great-aunt's legendary cannoli
* the latest MAC, Stila, or BeneFit lipstick color
* CD of his/her choice—Old Crooners, New Age, Alt Rock
* Playstation NBA game
* tickets to the Stones reunion tour
* a box of fine cigars

Other Landlord Heel-pinchers

* Pay your deposit in crisp hundred-dollar bills rather than a boring old check—and add an extra hundred or two.
* Offer to pay three months' rent up front if you can.
* If you have any famous relatives, bring them along.
* If you don't have any famous relatives, pretend you do. (Works equally well whether you have an unusual or common last name.)

Note to Self: If you wait to get what you want, it may be too late.

where. It must have enough room for a Palme d'Or or two and a handful of Oscars,

Roommate Revenge!

Getting the place of your dreams might mean acquiring the roommate of your nightmares. An unrelenting series of covert attacks could get you the upper hand and maybe even the bigger bedroom. But beware—you have 24/7 access and so does your roommate.

* Replace your roommate's powdered detergent with powdered bleach.

* Fill out a change-of-address form and send his/her mail to Bolivia.

* Hide his/her bills until they're past due.

* If your roommate borrows your car, call the police, report that your car was stolen, and give the cops your roommate's physical description.

* Record over all of his/her favorite videos with *Larry King Live.*

* Use a razor blade to cut out the last 10 pages of the novel he/she is reading.

* While you have that razor blade handy, gently slice a few stitches in the butt seam of all his/her jeans.

* Replace creme rinse with Nair.

* Call AA, Overeaters Anonymous, Planned Parenthood, the Forum, and the Church of Scientology to request that information be sent to your roommate's work address.

* Fill his/her Listerine with bourbon.

Make Your Pad a Palace in Three Easy Steps

Whether you live in a Park Avenue penthouse, a split-level ranch with four roommates, or a 1978 Ford Pinto, you should know how to turn your pad into a bad girl palace. If you've landed your dream pad and have the budget to decorate it just the way you want, skip ahead to the next section. If not, stay tuned.

Transforming your home into the perfect pad is an easy three-step process—cleanse, exfoliate, decorate!

Step one: Cleanse!

Even the dumpiest dump looks 100 percent better when it's clean—and 1,000 percent better when it's cleaned by someone else. If you can't afford a maid, figure out which one of your friends is a compulsive cleaner (there's one in every bunch!) and bribe, beg, or barter to get her to clean for you. If that doesn't work, arrange to co-host a dinner party with two or three good girl types at your place once a month. The deal—you host, they clean afterward. (Be sure to hold your big bad girl party—where people had food fights, puked, and spilled drinks—previous to this one.)

If you're stuck doing the dirty work yourself, you'll want to develop some time-saving techniques to maximize your efficiency.

and of course have a town house in a beautiful city.   I want to be healthy, happy,

Instead of sweeping with a broom, use a hair dryer like one of those big leaf blowers and corral all the filth and fuzz into a shopping bag in a corner, or blow it into your housemate's room and just close the door.

Cluttered tabletops? Don't waste time sorting through things—just wipe the mess into a big garbage bag in one arm's sweep, then stash the bag in a closet. If you haven't missed anything after a month, throw the whole bag away.

Vacuum cleaner on the fritz? Spray yourself with hair spray and roll back and forth on the carpet until it's clean.

If you wear those exfoliating skin gloves on both hands, you can scrub the tub and tile in half the time. Be sure to stand inside the tub barefoot while cleaning. The harsh bathroom products will eat away your calluses and rough, dry skin better than any pedicure!

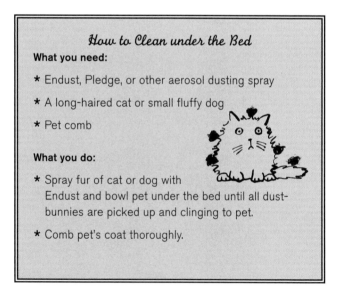

How to Clean under the Bed

What you need:

* Endust, Pledge, or other aerosol dusting spray

* A long-haired cat or small fluffy dog

* Pet comb

What you do:

* Spray fur of cat or dog with Endust and bowl pet under the bed until all dust-bunnies are picked up and clinging to pet.

* Comb pet's coat thoroughly.

strong, and full of piss and vinegar. I want my breasts to not fall any more than

Things to Do with . . .
Your Trendy Impulse Buys

* **crocheted mini poncho:**
  drape over a lamp shade to set the mood
  or wear as an off-the-shoulder pot holder

* **drawstring cargo clam diggers:**
  emergency flotation device or high-fashion neck
  wrap/lunch bag

* **polar fleece bikini:**
  cut into bathtub scouring pads or just wear and
  shimmy around in the tub with cleanser

* **micro cardigan:**
  gift for your four-year-old niece

* **hooded blazer:**
  begin career as business-to-business stalker

* **rhinestone hair clip:**
  fab roach clip for weddings or formal affairs

* **mesh sports bustier:**
  relocate to kitchen for straining pasta or holding
  ripe fruit

* **power bead bracelets:**
  restring into taxi driver–style seat cover

* **platform high-top sneakers:**
  fill with plaster of paris
  and use as bookends

* **smog-colored nail polish:**
  touch up nicks and scratches on neighbors' cars

* **shrug:**
  make a hole for the tail and you've got a chic butt-
  warmer for your dog

they already have. I want a boyfriend who cleans the toilet. I want to be a balle-

Things to Do with . . .
Photos of Your Evil Ex

* Dartboard bull's-eye.

* Write embarrassing sexual stats on back, laminate, and trade with all your friends.

* Pop a bunch into the Cuisinart and turn into confetti for your next New Year's party.

* Mail off to inmates in local prisons with a touching and titillating letter of introduction. (Include your ex's return address and phone number, of course.)

* Use packing tape to adhere to soccer balls, baseball bats, or bowling balls.

* Spread one inch apart on ungreased cookie sheet and broil on high.

* Stick to grille of car to catch high-speed bug splats.

* Bury in backyard with a dead fish.

* Build a desperate loser's website to help him meet new chicks.

* Drain toilet and superglue photo to bottom of toilet bowl.

* Line the bottom of your birdcage or cat litter box.

rina. I want the body of a ballerina. I want to date a male ballerina. I want to be

Step two: Exfoliate!

Before you can feel at peace in your home, you have to exfoliate emotionally by shedding all the crap that collects in corners, drawers, and the back of your fridge and makes you feel yucky. Unflattering photos of yourself should be the first to go. Next throw out newspapers a week old, magazines three months old, unpaid bills six months old, and anything in the fridge covered with mold. Be ruthless, be fearless, be bold. Any photos of your evil ex-boyfriend, ugly old bridesmaid dresses, or troubling trendy impulse buys—out!

Step three: Decorate!

Sick of feeling like you live in a Pottery Barn catalog? Saddened to find that the Ikea stuff you just bought is already in someone else's dumpster? Then it's time to start decorating like bad! Your pad should reflect your personality and your own unique bad girl style.

You don't need an interior decorating budget to create fabulous one-of-a-kind designer pieces for your home. Just take a good look around your place to spot the crap you have in simple abundance—past-fashionable impulse buys, magazines and catalogs, Chinese food containers, dry-cleaning bags, old pantyhose. These are your raw materials for creating disposable home furnishings and decorative accent pieces. And if you spill red wine, or your cat pukes on something, or you get sick of it all, just throw it away or set it on fire!

Remember: Decorating with those high–price tag items you no longer use will help you transition gradually and relieve guilt as well.

able to afford to go to the ballet. I want to take long walks on the beach, ski fast

More Junky-to-Funky Decorating Ideas

It's easy to make distinctive home furnishings with a little creative ingenuity and access to a thriving recycling bin or dumpster. When you transform junk into funk, you'll make your pad look chic and Martha Stewart want to shriek. And who doesn't want that?

* Fill a Hefty garbage with Styrofoam packing peanuts, tie bag securely, and you've got a beanbag chair! (Prick a few dozen holes with a pin to increase the life expectancy of your chair.)
* Wallpaper your bathroom with take-out food menus.
* Old pantyhose draped over the curtain bar create a soft, gauzy window treatment your neighbors will envy.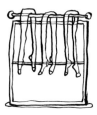
* Stuff wadded-up dry-cleaning bags into jumbo Ziploc bags to create space-age throw pillows.
* Glue all those wine bottle corks to the wall behind your bed to make a headboard that doubles as a bulletin board.
* Cover your bedroom walls with jumbo bubble wrap for that comforting padded-cell effect.
* Bubble wrap also makes snappy seat covers for dining room chairs.
* An old door from a car or refrigerator that you find at the dump or on the street makes a groovy coffee table or wall hanging.
* Make coffee tables, nightstands, or end tables out of stacks of home-furnishing catalogs.

Note to Self: Just because it's free doesn't mean you want it.

down some hills and occasionally jump for joy. I want a Wednesday night phone

Bad Girl Inventions We've Been Waiting For

A Phone Breathalyzer
This handy snap-on filter hangs up for you when you're tanked, preventing those embarrassing late-night drunken calls that you regret or forget in the morning.

Dating Insurance
A comprehensive policy that covers you, your ego, and your heart in the event of bodily injury, property damage, or unpleasant collisions while on a date.

Dial 9 for Wake-up Kiss
Forget those startling hotel wake-up calls that leave your heart pounding with fear. What you really want when you're alone on a business trip and far from home is a heart-pounding series of gentle wake-up kisses from a cute bellman with sweet lips. Now that's room service!

Oprah's Bookie Club
When Oprah picks your horse, you know you've got a sure thing!

Marriage Vacation Days
Just two to three weeks a year of no-questions-asked vacation time away from your husband and kids is all you really need to keep your sanity, your sex appeal, and your bad girl membership card. Is that too much too ask?

Viagra Blocker
Why spend the best years of your life staring at a four-hour hard-on, unless you really want to?

Zen Home: The Beginner's Guide

Regardless of your budget or lifestyle, your home should be a safe and sacred zone where you can relax, rejuvenate, and find a sense of inner peace.

The Home Beauty Shrine

Every woman should feel like the queen-bee sex goddess of love in her own home. If you're not quite there, don't despair. Simply transform your home into a personal beauty shrine in six easy steps.

1. Replace all harsh, unflattering lighting with candles.
2. Cover up every mirror with skinny mirrors. (Any super cheap mirror will do.)
3. Throw out your scale—it's not a bad girl item.
4. Keep at least one burned-out light bulb in bathroom, especially the one over the mirror.
5. Collect photos of yourself that you really love in various stages of undress and build a personal shrine to your individuality and beauty.
6. Burn a little incense and every fashion magazine you own at your altar.

call for a Saturday night date. I want my father to be able to communicate. I

Open Your Heart

Take an inventory of the little things that drive you nuts in your home and open your heart and mind to them. Invite these things into your life. When your heart is open and full of love, those common household annoyances can actually become your spiritual guides, assisting you on the path to heightened self-awareness.

When your heart is closed	When your heart is open
annoying running toilet	*a calming, burbling stream, gently flowing through your personal space like a vital life force*
drippy faucet	*relaxing rhythmic beat to guide your deep-breathing exercises, reminiscent of a rain forest after a light shower*
loud moaning radiator	*a meditation partner to accompany you and inspire your "Om" mantra*
creaky bedspring	*doubles as peaceful alarm clock every time you roll over, especially helpful for interrupting sleep to write in dream journal*
stinky litter box	*a soothing Zen garden where you can rake wave-like patterns around the stones with a large fork*

want to go to New Orleans for Mardi Gras. I want to be Nancy Drew. I want every

Creating the Illusion of a Home-Cooked Meal

If you want to cook a fabulous, delicious meal for your date or your friends, that's your problem. There are tons of books out there that tell you how to do it. Fortunately, this isn't one of them.

The truth is, no one ever wants to see the hostess working up a sweat in the kitchen. Guests feel guilty or intimidated, or they start wondering about your personal hygiene and how many months your sponge has been in your life. In fact, no one wants to see the hostess working at all—which is damn good news for you if you don't want to cook.

1. Place your food delivery order.
2. Make sure you have about a week's worth of dirty dishes and pots and pans in the sink. Leave them there.
3. Sign for the food delivery.
4. Splatter dots of sauce (whatever comes free with your order) over stove, on wall near stove, and on your outfit.
5. Transfer food to your own down-home, chipped or stained serving bowls, platters, or casserole dishes. Old dishes make it seem more plausible.
6. Pop in a warm oven or microwave.

Pay Attention to Detail

If you're a real overachiever, buy an onion, some garlic, and a bag of fresh herbs. Sauté some onion and garlic until they're lightly browned and a heavy aroma hangs in the air. Dump sauté in garbage and add dirty pan to pile. Before your dinner guests arrive, stash the bag of mixed herbs outside—if you don't have a bush to tie it to, tape the bagged herbs to back porch or fire escape. As you're putting the finishing touches on the meal, say in a clear, loud voice, "Let me just cut some fresh herbs from my herb garden." Then step outside or lean out onto the fire escape and pluck a few herbs from the bag.

Note to Self: Do not eat beans or spicy foods before a massage.

teach English class in a push-up bra and with my hair in a bun. I want to have sex

Getting a Great Table (without Reservations)

No dinner reservations? No reservations about playing "Let's pretend"? No problem! It's 7:45 on a Friday night. What do you do? Just think like a bad girl, play drop a name, and you'll be sipping a vintage cuvée at the best table by 8:00.

Drop a Foodie Name

Whether you live in a big city, a small town, or a small town that thinks it's a big city, the foodies are an incestuous, competitive, passionate, gossipy bunch. And this is good. (Foodies are the people in the restaurant community—the restaurateurs, the chefs, the career waiters, and all the people who love them or sleep with them.) All you have to do to secure a great table is drop one foodie's name at another foodie's restaurant.

The trick is figuring out which name to drop where. It's a safe bet simply to read the paper and stay up on the latest foodie news. If a new restaurant opens and gets a fab review, pick any one the foodies mentioned in the article. (This could backfire given the probable jealousy factor. But hey. You never know until you try.) Never pretend to be a foodie—it's too risky! Most know what the others look like, even if they've never actually met. Instead just drop a name and pretend to be his or her girl

on my desk knowing that someone could walk in at any moment.   I want my

Friday (wink, wink). Alternatively, you might be a dear old friend visiting from out of town—"They said my visit just wouldn't be complete without a meal here, since it's absolutely the best dining experience in town."

Drop a Restaurant Reviewer Name

Never pretend to be a local restaurant reviewer. (They never give their real names.) But you can pretend to be writing the restaurant section for a travel guide. Say something like, "Hi, I'm reviewing restaurants for the next Let's Go/Virgin/Rough Guides/Lonely Planet guide to [city name]." If they ask for a business card, scoff, sneer, and say, "Do I look like a corporate slave? I'm freelance, duh." Better yet, whip out this book and say, "I'm covering the restaurant scene in [city name] for the *Bad Girl's Guide to* [city name]. It's a new series of travel books. Very big deal, very hush-hush."

Drop a Celebrity Name

Read the paper in advance and figure out who's in town—a visiting pro team, a fab dance troupe, a film production crew. Then, five minutes before you go, call from your cell phone or a nearby pay phone and drop a visiting big shot's name, throw in a few relevant details, and you'll be in.

"Hello, I'm calling for the Paltrow party. Can you squeeze in six in about 10 minutes? I know Gwyneth will really appreciate it."

Nobody checks ID for a reservation. If they give you a hard time, just say, "We're the first ones here. He/she must still be signing autographs. We'll go ahead and sit down."

boyfriend to fantasize about me when he jerks off.   I want to watch my boyfriend

Bad Girl Confessions

Bad Girl Confession #16

In college, I lived with a bunch of neurotic women who were always dieting and obsessing about their weight. I couldn't stand it any longer so I dumped out their can of fat-free protein powder and filled it with Weight Gain 2000.

Bad Girl Confession #17

I was out drinking with a bunch of high school friends, and we pulled into an alley to go to the bathroom. We were standing around the car when a man pulled down his pants and exposed himself. I chased him. In his haste and surprise, his wallet fell out of his pocket. I picked it up and kept it for a week. Then I wrote an "exposing" letter to his wife and enclosed a photocopy of almost everything in his wallet. I turned his wallet in to the police—after removing all the cash.

Bad Girl Confession #18

I was trying on clothes with a friend. We got into a crazy, uncontrollable laughing fit and I peed in a dressing room at Nordstrom.

Bad Girl Confession #19

My roommate and I fake diabetes attacks to get seated quickly at restaurants.

Something
for Almost Nothing

Don't let a tight budget get you down!

Budget Beaters

Bad Girl's Sauna

Can't afford a health club at all but want the spa treatment? Just wrap yourself in a bath towel and stretch out in a hot car for two to three hours in the middle of summer with all the windows rolled up. Be sure to drink plenty of water, just as you would in a regular sauna.

Bad Girl Logic

Shop like a wild woman at sample sales or those crazy department store free-for-alls where everything is 50 to 70 percent off. If you buy enough, you'll save more money than you spend, which means you actually earned money shopping!

Bad Girl's Personal Trainer

No extra cash to get your butt in shape—and no motivation? Call around to every gym in town for a trial membership—and of course decline once the freebie is up. This a great chance to see which gym boasts the biggest babes. Continue making the rounds until someone recognizes your game. Then get a wig.

jerk off. I want to have sex in a kiddie pool full of tapioca. I want to bake bread,

Easy Money

How to make quick cash on the fly, bad girl style.

Bad Girl Bouncer

Set up a bar stool outside an almost trendy bar on a Friday or Saturday night and pretend to be the bouncer. (It helps to have a big, burly accomplice.) Check some people's ID, tell everyone there's a five-dollar cover charge, and don't let anyone enter until you get it. If you "card" people you know are well over 30, you're golden. They'll be so flattered, giggly, and delirious that they'll be thrilled to pay you five dollars just for the experience.

Bad Party Girl

Throw a huge party with a theme name like Lipstick Not Bombs—nothing too serious or nobody will come. Invite every person you've ever met, tell everyone it's a fund-raiser for a needy charity, and charge 10 bucks a head. Buy a jumbo bag of tortilla chips and some bean dip and have a cash bar or a keg of really cheap beer. Keep the lights turned low and the music volume cranked high. No one ever has to know that the needy charity is you!

Bad Girl Service

Make friends with a jovial bunch of well-lubricated drinkers in a wickedly crowded bar. Talk them up, tell your best jokes, swap dating stories. When the drinks get low, announce that you'll brave the jam-packed bar to get the next round. If someone hands you a twenty, take it—and head straight out the door. (Works great at private parties too: "Hey, I'm making a beer run!")

then eat it warm from the oven with fresh cream butter.   I want to inspire a man

Miracle Multitasking

You'll never feel better about yourself than when you're getting two things done at once! With a little bit of planning, you can save time and perfect the art of multitasking.

Miracle Multitasking	Result
Read the book while watching the movie.	Feel like a speed-reader.
Hang up while dialing.	Save money on phone bills.
Eat while going to the bathroom.	Lose weight.
Pay bills while shopping online.	Pay bills on time.
Drive there and back without stopping.	Feels like a road trip.
Paint nails while talking on cordless phone.	Feel beautiful and popular.
Puke while binge drinking.	Never get a hangover.
Break up on the first date.	Saves time and avoids upset.

to create art. I want to be the US ambassador to Portugal. I want to be a real

Parking Place Princess

A bad girl always finds a place to park—even if it's on the sidewalk. The only sure way to great parking karma is by praying to Gladys, the universal parking goddess. If you do, you'll find a parking place within seconds. Guaranteed. While you drive, just hold one hand flat above the steering wheel and move it around and around. As you do this, say the following three times out loud:

Gladys, Gladys, full of grace
Help me find a parking place.

Conscientious Parking Objector

Even when you can find a parking place, there will be times when you can't find a quarter or a good reason to pay because you're feeling like a conscientious objector protesting the senseless war against free parking. Either way, you've got options:

★ Most parking meters will stick in the yellow "Broken" position if you put a quarter in and then turn the knob only halfway (perfect for running a few quick errands).

★ Just in case that doesn't work, always keep a large brown shopping bag underneath the seat in your car with "broken" scribbled across the front. **Note to Self:** Do not yell, "Have a donut, fattie!" at cops to prove to friends you're sober enough to drive home.

writer. I want fewer, better clothes. I want a true love. I want to be a Solid Gold

Ticket Scalping

If you do get a parking ticket, don't get mad, get bad. Look around and find another car parked illegally or with an expired meter. Then slip your ticket under the windshield wiper. Most responsible, financially stable people will just pay the damn thing without examining it. But if they don't pay it, no big whoop. You'll get a courtesy reminder in a few weeks. And if you do choose the right type of car, you're off the hook. No tickey, no problem.

Ticket Switcheroo

If you're going to be parked illegally for a long time and suspect you may get a ticket, keep your eyes peeled for any other car parked near you with a fresh ticket. Just yank the ticket off that windshield and slap it on yours!

How to Make a VIP Parking Pass

Find an image of two hands clasped together in prayer. Photocopy it, enlarging or reducing it to about four inches in length. Print "VIP Parking Permit—Official God Business" in large black scroll across the top of a white piece of 8½ x 11" paper. Fold paper in half. Center the hands-in-prayer image on the half page and tack with rubber cement. Then laminate.

Whenever you can't find a legal place to park, just pull over wherever and toss this VIP parking pass on the dashboard. No God-fearing mortal will ticket you or have you towed. And how can they dispute your parking pass? After all, we're all here on official God business, aren't we?

dancer. **I want a country house with a garden and a lap pool.** **I want a step-**

Airline Upgrades

These days, it's almost impossible to get upgraded to first class—almost. If you're a bad girl, you're chances are better than most for landing one of them without paying a penny. You have two strategies: You can work the frazzled agents at the ticket counter or gate, or you can work a flight attendant once you're on board. (If there are seats available, this can actually be more effective.) Each strategy requires a different approach. But hey, if you strike out at the gate, then you get a second chance on board. Regardless of your strategy, be imaginative, be fearless—and be someone other people will want to help. Translation: always a bad girl, never a bitch.

The Compassionate Insider

When approaching the ticket counter or gate to check in, smile warmly at the agent and say something like, "Hi. So, how are the angry masses treating you today?" Acknowledge whatever response you get, then say, "I know how it is. I used to be a flight attendant for United/American/Delta" (whatever airline you're not flying that day). The next question will most likely be, "Where were you based?" Your answer, "Chicago. It was rough; I was always on reserve. I spent more time **deadheading** on a **jumpseat** than I did working, so I don't care what seat you put me in now that I'm a passenger. I'm

mother I could actually love and respect.   I want unsquelchable laughing fits sev-

just so happy to have a real seat!"

(**Deadheading:** When crew member rides on a flight to another city to cover a flight that originates there. **Jumpseat:** Those uncomfortable little pull-down seats that flight attendants sit on during takeoff and landing.)

If you're humble, grateful, charismatic, and convincing, some airline agents will reward you with a first class seat if they have one available. And you won't even have to ask.

The Giddy Fiancé

The situation: You're flying with a man to someplace exotic—Rome, Paris, Sydney, Hong Kong. Just after boarding, sneak over to a flight attendant. (Look for a gay male or a happy female with a wedding band who looks like she's getting some action. Avoid older divorcees, or any cranky woman who is more likely to be jealous than excited for you.)

The story: (whispering and panting with excitement while jumping up and down) "Oh my God! I think my boyfriend is going to propose on this flight! I felt the ring box in his pocket! Oh my God! Oh my God! Oh my God! Is there any way you could let us sit in first class? It would be sooooo perfect! It would be soooooo romantic! Please? Please? Oh paleeeze?"

After you've had your fill of free champagne, either play out the charade or stage a little faux fight, and throw a drink in your man's face.

eral times a day. I want beautiful salt and pepper hair. I want a bike with a

That Bastard!

The situation: You're flying alone, going anywhere, and seated near a lovey-dovey couple, ideally an older man with a younger woman. Just after boarding, sneak over to a flight attendant. (Look for a gay male or an unhappy female with or without a wedding band who looks like she's not getting any action.)

The story: (whispering and fuming with rage while spitting bile) "I can't believe that bastard! See that disgusting excuse for a human being over there? He's married to my best friend, who's at home going through her second round of chemo. Can you believe him? That pig! That bastard! If I have to watch him with that floozy for an entire flight, I'm going to clobber him with a tray table and strangle him with my headphones!"

If the flight attendant doesn't get the hint, lunge toward the happy couple growling like a pit bull. That usually does the trick.

Note to Self: Ignore tempting offers of free airfare, lodging, and meals. When it's family, it's no vacation.

banana seat. I want a voice like Ella Fitzgerald. I want people to do skits about

Things to Do with . . .
Your Old Bridesmaid Dresses

* Drench with ketchup and dress up as Carrie for Halloween.

* Open a museum of unnatural history.

* Memorable costumes for your all-girl band.

* Donate to the local high school drama department.

* Throw a Bridesmaid Beauty Pageant for your friends, with prize categories like "Most Reflective," "Biggest Butt Bow," and "All-around Ugliest."

* Crash the local prom and hit on 17-year-old hotties.

* Cut off and wear as a cocktail dress. (Yeah, right!)

* Leave all of them in your unlocked car until stolen and take a huge tax deduction.

* Sew into board bags for your snowboard and surf-board.

* Sell on eBay.

* Make your bridesmaids wear them in your wedding.

me on Saturday Night Live. I want to be seduced by a stranger. I want a guaran-

190

teed orgasm every time I take the time to undress.   I want my grandmother to

Stay Tuned . . .

What you want is constantly changing, just as you are. So keep asking yourself, keep checking your pulse for pleasure, and keep your eyes on the prize—fun! You don't have to know what you want for the rest of your life to go after it, you only have to know what you want right now. Get into the swirl. You're a bad girl!

live forever.   I want to have bigger muscles than my boyfriend for just one day

About the Author

Cameron Tuttle is the author of the best-selling *Bad Girl's Guide series* and *The Paranoid's Pocket Guide,* all from Chronicle Books. She gets what she wants in San Francisco.

About the Illustrator

Susannah Bettag's mind-tingling illustrations have appeared in magazines like *Seventeen* and *Ms.* as well as in *The Bad Girl's Guide to the Open Road.* She lives in San Francisco.

Go to badgirlswirl.com to reach the author and illustrator and to mix it up with other bad girls.

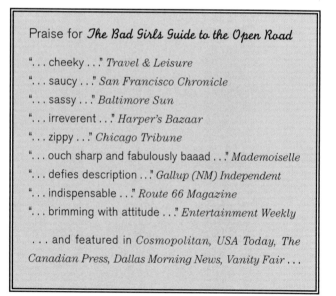

Praise for *The Bad Girls Guide to the Open Road*

". . . cheeky . . ." *Travel & Leisure*

". . . saucy . . ." *San Francisco Chronicle*

". . . sassy . . ." *Baltimore Sun*

". . . irreverent . . ." *Harper's Bazaar*

". . . zippy . . ." *Chicago Tribune*

". . . ouch sharp and fabulously baaad . . ." *Mademoiselle*

". . . defies description . . ." *Gallup (NM) Independent*

". . . indispensable . . ." *Route 66 Magazine*

". . . brimming with attitude . . ." *Entertainment Weekly*

. . . and featured in *Cosmopolitan, USA Today, The Canadian Press, Dallas Morning News, Vanity Fair . . .*

so I could beat him at arm wrestling.   I want to drive a pickup.   I want sex.